PRAISE FC ~ ~..... /// AWAKENING.

"We are perfectly imperfect! A great opening for a book that is truly that—perfect in all its humanity. I am a huge Sam Liebowitz fan and think everyone should keep this book by their bedside. You'll laugh, you'll cry. You'll pick it up whenever you can't sleep."

Teresa de Grosbois, Best-selling Author of *Mass Influence*

"This book is filled with practical reminders on how to live a fulfilled and happy life. So grateful to Sam for putting his heart into this gift to humanity."

Jennifer Hough, President, TheWideAwakening.com

"The path on the journey of life offers you countless twists and turns. If you pay close attention, you will walk away with a few exquisite lessons and experience treasured pearls of wisdom. *Everyday Awakening* captures these soul stories in a beautiful way. If you're seeking a guide to transform your daily walk, this is the book for you."

Lisa Marie Platske, Best-selling Author, Founder, Upside Thinking, Inc. & Design Your Destiny Live

"When I was a much younger man and trying to figure my way out of a dysfunctional past, I read a book that really helped me. I was so grateful that the author took the time and the care to put these thoughtful gems on paper so I could benefit. I had the exact same feeling of gratitude when I read Sam's new book. It captures the deep (and practical) wisdom that we can all use in our lives—and it's in the perfect bite-sized format that you can read daily. Do yourself a favor and get this book!"

Ganz Ferrance, Ph.D., Psychologist,
Author of *The Me Factor*

"This book is deeply intuitive and pragmatic with countless emotional aspects that may get in our way. So much is covered, from fear to grief, loss, and countless other issues. More importantly, Sam gives us a way out—or is it an easy way *in?* His deep insights guide us to a place of graceful inner transformation. He's done the heavy lifting for us all in a very digestible way. Bravo, Sam, for making it easier for us to navigate the pitfalls of life. Namaste."

Gary Stuart, Best-selling Author,
Master Constellation Healing Facilitator

"Living your dream life is possible when you know how powerful you are. I love the messages that remind me who I am, what I stand for, and how I can make a difference. Sam Liebowitz now feels like a trusted soul friend whom I can lean upon at any time by simply picking up this book."

Laura Rubinstein, C.Ht., Best-selling Author,
Chief Digital Marketer, Transform Today

"Sometimes you just need a moment to reset and come back to center. I found *Everyday Awakening* the perfect life-affirming pick-me-up for doing just that. This go-to collection of pearls of wisdom will truly touch your soul."

Valerie René Sheppard, Self-mastery Expert, Author of
the Award-winning, #1 Best-seller *Living Happy to Be ME!*

"A delightful compilation of insightful suggestions for dealing with the kinds of thoughts everyone has, and our common human queries. It's a great, great read that will inspire you and fill you with wonder and joy. It's also an opportunity to slow down and reflect on who you really are! Get this book. You might want to buy multiple copies for gifts for family and friends. It is a joy to read."

Maureen St. Germain, Founder of Akashic Records International, COVR Award-winning Author of *Opening Your Akashic Records* & *Waking Up in 5D*

"Powerful words of wisdom and healing. Sam Liebowitz shines a clear light on personal growth and brings powerful perceptions that open you to new ways of thinking and being. As you read these short chapters, you can move into a higher place with clarity, joy and awakening. This is a gift for us all!"

Lumari, Intuitive Life Coach, Creative Catalyst, Channel, & Award-winning, Best-selling Author

"A fellow seeker with grounding and sacred collective wisdom. Sam Liebowitz eloquently captures the understanding that the inward journey leads to daily awakening, happiness, and joy."

Terry Wildemann,
Mindset, Leadership, & Business Accelerator

"Sam is one of the most sincere, real people I have ever met. I instinctively trusted him the moment we met, and that trust has only deepened. It is heart that characterizes him most to me and that is the quality so evident in *Everyday Awakening.* As Sam puts it 'The greatest dance we do is the dance between head and heart.' Indeed, he has mastered that dance as few have. This book captures in words the soul of a beautiful and wise man and I know it will be a great companion to you, providing insight, comfort, and soul nourishment for many years to come."

GP Walsh, Spiritual Teacher & Author,
The Tao of Allowing and *Tapping on the Buddha*

"If someone were to ask me, 'What do you recommend to nourish your soul?' I would say read this book. It contains profound reminders of conscious thoughts that inspire, uplift, and remind me who I really am and the true essence of my soul's path. Thank you, Sam, for this treasure trove of wisdom."

Karen McGregor, International Speaker, Best-selling Author
of *The Tao of Influence*, Founder, Speaker Success Formula

"Sam's book is both an easy read and deeply profound. It's honest, it's thought-provoking, and even if you incorporate just one of Sam's 126 lessons into your life, I guarantee a powerful shift for the better. Whatever you're creating or dreaming of creating, just close your eyes and randomly open to any page, and the solution will be there. That's what I did when I first got my copy and it left me speechless! If you're looking for knowledge for the next step on your journey, look no further than Everyday Awakening."

Debra Poneman, Bestselling Chicken Soup Author
& Founder of Yes to Success, Inc.

"Sam is a super-mensch—a big-hearted, mindfully engaged, tireless advocate with a third eye for business. He has taken his many wide-ranging gifts, talents, and stories, keenly honed over many years, to create an empowering and uplifting book for people who want to know how to move forward in a world that seems lost. Don't worry, Sam is here to show you how to move confidently into the new normal as it emerges, which is filled with great opportunity if you know how to look for it."

Whitney Vosburgh, Fortune 20 Chief Marketing Officer, Coauthor of the *Work The Future! Today* Book Series

"With his book *Everyday Awakening,* Sam Liebowitz has gifted us a daily contemplation from his own deep roots in spiritual practice. Whether you are just beginning the spiritual journey, or many marathons into your exploration, this book offers prompts to help you go deeper within yourself."

Kerri Hummingbird, Soul Guide, Best-selling Author of *The Second Wave*

"*Everyday Awakening* is one of those books to leave on your nightstand to read over and over. This compendium of blog posts will instantly touch your heart and soul and inspire you to dream new dreams. It is filled with such valuable insights and wisdom into the human condition that I recommend you give it as a gift to each person you love."

Jan Goldstoff, Publicist/Photographer, Golden Connector

"Reading Sam's book is like taking a break in the oasis of life. It helps me to be kinder to myself and it reminds me of what matters most. This is one of these precious books we want to read again and again. And every time we do, we discover more gems of wisdom, inspiration, and love. Read Sam's book and you will fall in love again with life and with yourself."

Monique Blokzyl, CEO & Founder, HeartPowered Business

Dear Kim,

May the words inside Hold you with the beauty, power, and love that love within you.

EVERYDAY AWAKENING

....

YOU ARE MORE POWERFUL THAN YOU KNOW

SAM LIEBOWITZ

THE CONSCIOUS
CONSULTANT

Sam Liebowitz / The Conscious Consultant
Website: www.TheConsciousConsultant.com

Ordering Information: Special discounts are available on quantity purchases by corporations, associations, and others. For details, contact the publisher at the address above.

Library of Congress Control Number 2020910654

Everyday Awakening / Sam Liebowitz —1st ed.

ISBN 978-1-7351973-0-2 (paperback)

CONTENTS

PART II: OUR GROWTH: DISRUPTION, PROGRESS, AND FLOW

PART III: OUR WILL: ENERGY, INTEGRITY, AND EMPOWERMENT

PART IV: OUR RELATIONSHIPS: CONNECTION, LOVE, AND COMMUNITY

**PART V: OUR TRUTH: STORY, WORDS,
AND VIBRATION**

PART VI: OUR VISION: AWARENESS, DISCERNMENT, AND INTENTION

PART VII: OUR WORLD: INSPIRATION, IMAGINATION, AND CONTRIBUTION

This book is dedicated to all the people who have supported me throughout the years—the ones who gave me the encouragement to keep moving forward just when I needed it the most, especially my family. Most importantly, I dedicate it to my wife, without whose support I never would have been able to create what you are reading right now.

INTRODUCTION

This is the first book I have ever written. It is roughly five years in the making. Not that I started off with the intention to write a book. I merely started writing a blog for the newsletter of my internet radio station. Twice a week at first, then, more recently, only once a week. Yet that effort over the years became something much more than I ever expected.

The idea to turn my over 300 blog posts into a book came from someone whose blog I read every day, Seth Godin. When he turned his blog into the beautifully formatted book *What to Do When It's Your Turn*, it inspired me to see if I could do the same thing. What you are holding in your hands is the result.

Whittling down my blog posts from over 300 to 126 posts was no easy task. I wanted to include them all, but that would not have been fair to you. There was some redundancy and there were many posts, especially the early ones, that just were not that good. What you have before you are the pieces of writing that have stood the qualitative and emotional test. I'll let you be the judge as to whether or not they are any good.

Although I took several creative writing classes in college and toyed with the idea of being a writer, I have never really written professionally. Because I'm an entrepreneur, of course, I have had to write many things over the years, such as content for my websites, advertisements for events I put on, descriptions of meetup groups I put together, and so forth. This is my first attempt to gather my writing and publish it.

I have organized the material into seven chapters, each related to one of the seven energy vortexes in the body that the Hindus refer to as *chakras*. I'm not going to go into what a chakra is here, but if you'd like to find out more, you can read Anodea Judith's book *Wheels of Life*. It is by far the one of the most comprehensive books on the chakras I have ever read.

My book is structured as follows:

- Part One is about the foundation of who we are as human beings.
- Part Two is about our growth, specifically creativity and dealing with change.
- Part Three focuses on our will, our energy, and how we organize our life.
- Part Four covers relationships, in particular our connection to ourselves, others, and the community at large.
- Part Five explores communication and the issue of speaking our truth.
- Part Six is on our vision and understanding of life.
- Finally, Part Seven is where we deal with purpose, inspiration, and our divinity.

Although this book can be read in sequence, it does not have to be. It is the type of book that you can just flip open to a random page on any given day to see what message chance has in store for you. The method of choosing your reading is rarely as random as you might think; most of the time the piece will be right on target for what you might be dealing with at the time. So, I invite you to be open to the mystery that is in the nonrandom randomness of life.

Please use this book to support you on your path, to find guidance when you need a signpost indicating where to go, and to learn more about how powerful and amazing you truly are. It is no accident that you are reading this book. You are who it was always intended for. My intention is that it will serve you well today, tomorrow, and for the foreseeable future!

PART ONE

OUR FOUNDATION

ESSENCE, PRESENCE, AND WELLBEING

1.

··

WE ARE PERFECTLY IMPERFECT

It is easy to fall into the trap of thinking that there is something wrong with us. It's not unusual to feel that we are broken and need to be fixed.

That is not the truth. Actually, we are perfect exactly the way we are.

This does not mean that we do not desire to do better. What it really is about is accepting ourselves exactly the way we are without judgment or criticism.

We all feel not good enough. We all feel unworthy.

The thing is: that's usually our greatest gift! It may seem counterintuitive, yet the very things we are trying so hard to change, are our greatest assets. We just have to learn how to reframe and reinterpret that part of our lives. Our faults and our flaws are what make us human. They make us relatable to other people. We can empathize with each other's pain.

Sure, we can learn to do better—and there is nothing wrong with wanting to improve. In fact, working on ourselves is the great work of a lifetime. Yet we don't have to judge ourselves in the process. Or others for that matter. We are not here to beat ourselves up or pick at every little mistake we make.

It is primarily through our mistakes that we learn and grow. There is nothing wrong with making a mistake. So, let's find a way to stop marinating in our misery and see ourselves as being perfectly imperfect. To celebrate our mistakes as much as we celebrate our successes.

Let's be not just a little kinder to ourselves, but a lot kinder! Life is meant to be joyful, not painful and demeaning.

Let's let our light shine even though the dark spots are visible. Being real is a lot easier than living up to some false ideal. Can you start to cut yourself some slack and not be so hard on yourself starting today?

2.

....

WE ARE NOT BROKEN, AND WE DON'T NEED TO BE FIXED

Sometimes we get a nagging feeling, an itch to change something about ourselves. As if we need to be fixed. There is that seminar to go to. Another course to take. Another book to read. And in trying to scratch that itch, we fall into the trap of the never-ending cycle of self-improvement.

We think:

I am broken and I need to be fixed.

There is something wrong with me.

Please fix me.

I am in pain so it must be my fault.

I did something wrong.

I always mess up.

I am just defective.

We may not say it. We may not even think it. Yet we act that way. Because we feel that we are not good enough in some way, we go looking for a guru or a teacher to make us feel better.

The trap is that we are looking for a solution outside of ourselves. We think that there must be someone out there who can change us.

Just one more workshop and I'll be okay.

Just one more boot camp and I'll be at peace.

The fallacy is the idea that we are broken and need to be fixed. For we are not broken. We don't need to be fixed. We are absolutely perfect the way we are. We are whole, complete, and enough.

Pain is normal. The real issue is the story we tell ourselves about it. The story about why we feel the way we do. The story about why that thing happened to us. The story that tells us there is something wrong with us.

What if there is not something wrong with us? What if that story is false? What if everything that happened to us is here to serve us? What if everything is perfect and we are perfect too—just learning our lessons and growing every day? What if the real issue is the story we made about the issue?

What if you don't need to go to another seminar, another bootcamp, to feel better? What if the only thing that prevents you from feeling better about yourself is you? If the stories don't serve you, there's no purpose in hanging on to them.

When we drop the stories, everything changes. When we let go of the stories, we can start fresh. We can start anew. And we can feel better about ourselves in an instant. We may not be able to drop the story right away, but is there a way for you to reinterpret the age-old story that has been haunting you to something a little kinder, a little gentler on yourself?

3.

....

LIFE HAPPENS FOR US, NOT TO US

We have all had a crisis in our lives, and when we do, we can feel like the whole world is against us. We can feel powerless in that situation, though nothing could be further from the truth. We can feel like victims. We can feel as if nothing we do makes any difference.

The real issue is not what happens. The real issue is our perspective. Our emotions can make us feel that life happen *to* us. Actually, life happens *for* us!

It's a small word. A tiny change in the sentence. Yet it makes all the difference.

Life happens *for* us, not *to* us.

So, what does that mean? How does changing that one little word help? It means that everything that happens is here to serve us in some way.

Maybe we can't see it in the moment—especially when we do not yet have some distance. With time, things begin to look different. Slowly, over time, what seemed like a horrible thing turns out to be our greatest gift. It may be a defining moment in our lives. It may be the very thing that launches us onto our new path. It may be the one thing that completely transforms the trajectory of our future.

How do we know? In the moment, we don't. Yet if we approach it with the perspective that it is happening for us, suddenly we find peace. We become the calm center in a chaotic storm. Our whole perspective shifts and we are more open to see other possibilities. We are the very person we need to be to see it through.

It may not seem like it at the time. It may feel like the greatest challenge we have ever faced. Or perhaps it is just a small inconvenience. Regardless of what it is, it is happening *for* us, not *to* us.

You don't have to believe it, just try it on. Does it help? Do you feel better? More empowered? Does that perspective serve you?

If it does, then why not use it? What's the worst that could happen to you if you do?

There is magic in life, and greater magic in believing and acting as if it all happens *for* us, not *to* us. Are you willing to try it on? Are you willing to test it out?

Try living as if life happens *for* you and see how you feel.

4.

....

WHEN WE FIND PEACE WITHIN, NOTHING CAN SHAKE OUR WORLD

When we feel at peace with ourselves, little can shake us. When we find our center, we are balanced and calm. This state is not about what life brings to us but about our ability to respond from a place of tranquility.

We often think that everything in our external world has to be calm for us to be calm. We feel that when life is hectic, with so many moving parts, we can't settle down. That if there is drama at work or in our relationships, we can't possibly be serene. Yet what is on the outside is not nearly as important as how we feel on the inside. If we have worked through most of our major trauma and our self-doubts, we change from the inside out.

When we come to accept ourselves for who we are, exactly as we are, how we feel on a daily basis changes. We no longer base our emotional state on what is happening around us. We can see things more clearly and not be rocked by our external circumstances. Because once we know we are okay, we are good, on the inside, then what happens on the outside is of far less importance to us.

We can be the eye at the center of the storm. We can be a rock for others when they are losing their heads over a crisis. We can be a calming influence in an emergency.

Our stillness does not mean we don't care. Our peacefulness is merely an indication of our understanding of how life works. For when we come to peace within ourselves, we see peace in the world around us. Things no longer have to be perfect once we understand that we are perfect, even with all our flaws. What keeps you from finding peace within yourself? Perhaps once you explore it you will find the peace you crave.

5.

....

WORKING HARD IS NOT THE ANSWER—UNLESS WE ARE WORKING HARD ON OURSELVES

Being ready to receive takes more effort than we often realize because there are so many things in our lives that teach us not to receive.

From the time we are born we are taught to think just of giving. On top of that, we experience all kinds of things that make us feel unworthy. These programs can be subtle and deep-rooted. They can come from family, friends, school, religion, and society at large.

For instance, we are indoctrinated to believe that we have to work hard for everything that comes to us. That sometimes, even then, it does not come. That we have to sacrifice and suffer to get somewhere in our lives–sometimes without a single reward.

These programs are powerful and pervasive. They are also completely untrue.

Life will always support us. When we allow the treasures of life to come in, they do. Yet allowing them to come is the hardest part for most of us. It often comes only after doing the deep work of untangling those ancient programs that control our thinking, our energy, our choices.

These programs are so unconscious that we are not even aware of the decision we make that pushes the very things we want away.

The effort is not about working so hard to achieve some goal. The effort is about working hard to unravel the beliefs that to achieve the goal must take hard work.

This does not mean we don't take action.

We must.

Yet, if we take action after having changed our beliefs, it becomes so much more effective. Self-exploration may be difficult, yet it is always rewarding. Have you taken the time to explore your own beliefs? Your underlying programs? How you operate in the world? See what change can occur in your life when you bring a greater awareness to them.

6.

....

SHINING A LIGHT ON SHAME IS HOW WE BEGIN TO RELEASE IT

Shame is something we don't often speak about in polite company. It's a topic we avoid, perhaps because it is at the heart of so many of our challenges. Yet speaking openly about shame and bringing it to light is exactly what we need to do to heal the wounds.

We get shamed as children for the littlest things: for writing on the wall. For coloring outside the lines. For playing with fire. For not being as good at school or sports as our siblings or the other kids. All those little incidents of being chastised or shamed add up over time to an unconscious feeling of unworthiness and being broken. Those feelings permeate our life in so many ways, both in our personal life and our business life. We then spend the rest of our lives running to seminars and gurus looking for the magic that will fix us and make us whole.

What we don't see is that no one else can fix us. It's purely an inside job.

It's also not something that we can do overnight. These unconscious patterns were built up and reinforced over years so it will take us time to rewire our brains and our nervous systems.

The first step in the rewiring process is to recognize that some shame is there, and it is running our lives in many different ways. We need to shine a light on the dark corners of our psyches. Doing this in community, among a trusted group of people whom we know will support us through the process, is essential.

Exploring this core issue in community not only helps us, it also helps the rest of the community because shame is so universal in our society.

Are you ready to shine the light on your shame? Do you have a community in which to work on it? Find those your truly trust and ask them if they would want to explore this topic together.

7.

....

TRUE EVOLUTION IS ACCEPTING OUR FAMILY WITHOUT JUDGMENT

As adults, our family is our biggest teacher. The way they judge us means more to us than anyone else. Yet how we choose to show up in the midst of all of that says more about us than any other situation. It is a great opportunity to put our practices and patience to work.

When those closest to us push our buttons, how we respond shows our maturity. Who we are as individuals is revealed by our actions in these most trying of situations. We can forgive our friends and our coworkers for behavior that annoys us. Can we do the same for family?

Our family may still treat us as if we are ten years old. Can we respond as if we are no longer ten? We stress over how our parents and other relatives act. We would prefer they change. Can we learn to accept them exactly the way they are?

Can we be with our family without judgment even when they judge us?

Can we be kind to them even when they are not kind to us?

Can we be patient with them if when they are not patient with us?

The sign of our true evolution is when we can face those that we know better than anyone else on the planet, and still accept them without judgment and with love.

Can you find a place in your heart to accept your family, exactly as they are?

8.

··

OUR PHYSICAL AND EMOTIONAL HEALTH ARE INTERDEPENDENT

The connection between our emotions and bodies is much deeper than many people think. As humans, we have a tendency to disconnect the physical from the emotions we feel. We think that being upset or being happy has no effect on how our bodies function, yet the opposite is true. Our feelings are intricately intertwined with our physical bodies.

When we are stressed, when we are depressed, when we are frightened, our bodies internal mechanisms all shift. Our immune systems don't work as well and blood flows either more slowly or at an accelerated rate. Our digestion starts to shut down. Our breathing becomes shallower and less oxygen makes it into the bloodstream.

When we are joyful, happy, and content, our bodies respond by functioning quite well. The immune system works better, the blood flow to all of our organs is steadier, we breathe more deeply, and the whole body is nourished.

When we suppress our emotions, the body reacts as well. If we suppress and ignore our emotions over a long period of time, wherever we store those emotions in our bodies suffers from long-term stress, and disease begins to form. Advanced science is showing us that there is a direct correlation between our emotional and physical health.

So, if we genuinely want to be healthy throughout our lives, emotional health is essential. But how do we become emotionally healthy? By expressing our emotions in a safe environment and working through our ups and downs instead of hiding them. We do not have to act on them. Yet we cannot avoid feeling them and giving those feelings to have a voice allows us to release them.

We all need a safe space in which to express ourselves. Can you find one or two people you feel truly safe with and express yourself to them? A little talking and some real openness can go a long way.

9.

....

STRENGTH DOES NOT COME FROM FORCE, IT COMES FROM BEING VULNERABLE

Being strong is not about strength.

Being strong does not mean we are domineering.

Being strong is not about being forceful.

Being strong is about something far more powerful.

True strength comes from deep inside us, from having an intimate connection to our souls.

Strength is also the power that comes from seeing ourselves clearly. Strength is the knowing that through our choices and our intentions we are the creators of our world.

We are strong when we make conscious decisions in our lives. And we are strong when we refrain from using our strength. But we are strongest when we allow ourselves to be the most vulnerable.

True strength is the will to exercise our power as a force for good. Might only makes right when the might is used to uplift and support. It is easy to use our muscles to hurt another. It is too easy to use intimidation to control another. These are signs of weakness, not strength. It is far harder and more difficult to be a gentle giant than to be a bully.

The world does not need more cowards hiding behind the masks of power. The world needs more people who have the courage and strength to be true, honest, and authentic.

Real strength comes from being a real person. Real vulnerability comes from sharing our difficulties and our pain.

Can you share more of your true self with another? Can you find one person to tell something vulnerable to that you've never told anyone before?

....

10

FEELING SAFE IS ESSENTIAL FOR US TO GROW AND BE AUTHENTIC

Feeling *safe* is more important than we think.

Feeling *safe* is about more than our environment.

Feeling *safe* involves more than just the people we're surrounded by.

Feeling *safe* is essential for us to grow and be authentic.

Feeling *safe* is essential for us to heal if we feel damaged.

As human beings, we get shocked by many things. Our nervous systems respond to all sorts of stimuli. Someone yelling at us on the phone, for example, can be a disturbing experience and make us feel unsafe to do business with that person. A stranger's energy when they walk into the elevator with us can make us feel unsafe. A dark and deserted place can make us feel unsafe as well. But we can also feel unsafe with our family, our colleagues, or our clients.

What triggers one person may not be what triggers someone else. As individuals, we have different associations and experiences.

Do we really know when we make someone else feel unsafe? Conversely, are we aware of what we do for others that makes them feel safe?

Without feeling safe we cannot relax. Without feeling safe, we cannot allow ourselves to show how we really feel inside. Without feeling safe, we cannot begin healing. What we often overlook, however, is that we have to feel safe with ourselves first before we can feel safe with anyone else.

Sometimes, we don't even consider what situations we need to be in to feel safe.

Do we feel safe with our families?

Do we feel safe with our friends?

Do we feel safe in our work environments?

What is the solution when we don't feel safe? Change where we are. Change who we are with. Change what we are experiencing.

When we find a moment's peace, then we can begin to look at what we truly need to feel safe. When we are alone, and present to ourselves, then we can feel into our bodies and see where there is tension or concern. Knowing what we need to feel safe is important in helping us to know how to create safety for others.

If we would all keep in mind what it means to feel safe and to how to create safety around us, perhaps we could create a safer world.

Can you be a little kinder to the people around you? Can you be a little more sensitive to someone's reaction to you to sense their lack of safety? Maybe it is in their tone of voice or body language. Notice it, feel it. Think about what you would want to feel safe in the safe situation. A little consideration can go a long way.

11.

....

SITTING STILL ALLOWS US TO BE MORE PRESENT TO OURSELVES AND OTHERS

How are we present to ourselves? Can we sit still and just be aware of our feelings? Do we fidget and become restless in our seat looking for something to do?

How we are when we are by ourselves actually tells us a lot about ourselves. When we are at peace with ourselves, it is easy to sit and be still. When we are uncomfortable with some aspect of ourselves, it is hard to spend time alone.

When we take a moment to just breathe and relax, are we really relaxed?

Most of the time, we are not relaxed around ourselves. We need to be doing something or be engaged in a conversation. We look for some kind of distraction to take us away from how we are really feeling. Yet, if we take a moment to explore that feeling, instead of avoiding it, we can learn quite a bit. We can see more clearly where our work is. We can feel what it is that triggers us. We can discover what unresolved issues are rolling around inside of us.

It is not always comfortable to just sit with ourselves. In fact, it can be quite challenging. Yet the rewards are enormous.

And the practice itself is quite helpful. It gives us that moment of peace with which we can enter our day. It helps us to be more centered and grounded. It reminds us to be gentler and kinder with ourselves, and it calls us to be more present to everything in our lives.

Presence allows us to be more available to others, and to ourselves.

Can you make some space in your life to just sit and be with yourself on a regular basis?

12.

....

LONELINESS IS ABOUT
SEPARATION FROM OURSELVES

Being alone does not mean we are lonely. Being lonely does not mean we are alone. Loneliness is about separation—not separation from others, but from ourselves.

When we are connected to our true authentic nature, we never feel lonely. That's because, at the very heart and core of who and what we are, we are a connected, eternal spirit. To cultivate the connection to our soul, being alone serves us. It is much easier for us to connect to ourselves if there are no external distractions.

When we look deep inside, we may find some scary things, yet ultimately, if we go deep enough, we connect to our true divine nature. We can also find our divine nature by seeing it in others and connecting to them. Yet, more often than not, we use connecting to others as an excuse not to look inside.

Why is that? Perhaps it is because we consciously don't know what we'll find there. Perhaps it is because we fear all those things we have been suppressing will rise up. Perhaps it is because we just don't feel worthy.

And yet if we sit still, even for five minutes and close our eyes and feel what is inside of us, a whole new world opens up. It is a world that is rich and full of texture and feeling. A world full of connection and support.

Our loneliness comes from disconnecting from this rich inner world.

When was the last time you took the time to connect with yourself? How about sitting with yourself on a regular basis? Are you ready for that connection?

13.

....

WHEN WE FIND OURSELVES IN RESISTANCE, LIFE HAS ANOTHER PLAN FOR US

We often don't understand why we are not in flow. We think we are doing the right things and on the right path, and still we encounter resistance.

Then something shifts. We get into a different business or career, or we find a new spiritual teacher. We form an amazing relationship that takes us in a whole new direction. And then flow starts to happen again. Suddenly things work out with little or no effort. Doors open for us that we never knew where there. At which point, we scratch our heads and wonder, *How did I not know I was on the wrong path before?*

It's easy to think that you are doing fine and going in the right direction, because movement of any kind often feels good at the time. But life has plans for us, and it is often only when we shift into what life wants for us—instead of doing what we want to suit our own agenda—that we truly end up in flow.

How do we know when we are not in flow? It's easy. Check in. Is there resistance in your path? If there is, it's time to do something different. Don't know what that is? Just wait! Everything doesn't have to be resolved in a day. Patience will get you there.

Don't sweat being in the resistance. Rest in it. Wait it out. Once your life takes a turn, the resistance will disappear. Can you recognize where in your life your in resistance? Can you lean into and let it be if not let it go?

14.

....

A NIGHT OFF IS OUR RIGHT AS CONSCIOUS BEINGS

Taking time off is not always easy for us. There are so many demands on us from every direction: Our families, our jobs, our businesses, and our friends all seem to want something from us.

We may feel as if we have to work at something in order to deserve a night off. But this is not the case. This is societal programming. There is no reason we have to "earn" time off. There is no reason we have to "work" for it. We all deserve a night off just for being who we are.

In fact, the people who feel the need to earn time off are usually the ones who need it most. They are the ones who are always giving of themselves. They are the ones who are working the hardest.

Yes, being productive can be a good thing—unless we are so focused on being productive that it wears us down or causes us to sacrifice our health or our relationships.

For us to give from a powerful place we need to be well rested. We need to have our metaphorical cups overflowing. We need to feel joyful, happy, and energized by being alive. It is hard to feel that way when we are working all the time. It is hard to feel powerful when we are worn out. It is hard to give what others need when we are fatigued.

Taking a night off is essential. Taking a night off just to "be" is something we all need. In this modern world, we are so busy that we rarely have the time to be with ourselves. To breathe. To be quiet. To relax and disengage. Yet it is one of the most essential things we can do for our mental, physical, and spiritual health.

And when you get really comfortable taking a night off for no other reason than you want to, then you can try taking a whole day off for no other reason than that you want to!

15.

....

WE CAN CHOOSE OUR OWN
STANDARDS FOR SUCCESS

Does success in "the world" mean success in your life?

We have a tendency to measure our success by society's standards: Do we have a big house? A car? A spouse? Kids? And most importantly, a well-paying job or a successful business? Yet we can have all these things and still feel empty inside. We can have all the external trappings of a successful life and still feel unfulfilled and disconnected. We can still feel that we are not contributing enough to the world.

Conversely, we can have none of those measures that meet society's expectations and still achieve inner peace. We can engage in profound relationships, create community among likeminded people, and feel fulfilled and whole.

The real and more important question is: *What are our own standards by which we will measure success in our lives?*

Is it knowing ourselves on a deep level? Is it having a life free of responsibility and being able to travel the world? Is it living close to the land and learning how to grow your own food and be self-sufficient? Deciding what we ourselves want and not allowing the external world to dictate our dreams is perhaps the most important form of success we can achieve. Then the pursuit of our dreams is meaningful.

Have you look at your dreams lately? Are they your real dreams or are they something tainted by other people's opinions? If there was no one else to consider, would you still have the same dreams?

16.

······································

WE ALL NEED HELP NOW AND THEN

We all need to call for help sometimes. Not because we aren't capable or strong. Not because we are unable to deal with a situation. We call for help because other people have had different experiences than ours, and with different experience comes different insight, different skills, different strengths, and different weaknesses.

That difference is what makes us human.

That difference is what makes us unique.

Sometimes we don't like the difference. Sometimes that difference is scary. Yet, when we are in need of someone with that exact difference, we crave it. No one has what they need all the time throughout their entire life. We need teachers, mentors, and guides to help us as we walk along our own path.

Calling for help is a very human thing to do. When we call for help, we find that together we can achieve more. It makes the path we're walking easier to traverse.

We always have a choice. We can choose to suffer in silence, or we can ask for the support we need. And by asking for support, we give the other person an opportunity to give. This may be something they are craving.

Can you see where you need help and are afraid to ask for it? Can you find out why you don't want to ask? Can you ask for help anyway, no matter how uncomfortable it makes you feel?

17.

························

WHEN WE SURRENDER, LIFE
TAKES CARE OF ITSELF

Sometimes, when we feel like we're pounding our head against a wall, it's time to stop. If we take the time to reflect on it, we might find something is off.

We think the wall is on the outside. Yet it might just be that the wall is inside us.

We may feel that life is putting obstacles in our path. That things are just getting harder and harder for no reason. We may feel resistance all around us. And nothing may seem to be working out.

Perhaps that is the time life is telling us something. Perhaps that is the time to take a closer look inside to see where our resistance is. To find out where are we not *surrendering*.

Blockages in our lives are not generated by people and events in the external world. They are internal, energetic blockages that keep us from where we want to go. They are the signs that we have some resistance to receiving.

Or to giving.

Or perhaps we are just resistant to letting go of control. Thinking we know what's best. Yet our perspective is so limited.

Can we really know what is best for the future? Can we truly see what will happen in five, ten, or fifteen years?

Perhaps that disaster of a vacation will turn out to be the last time you spend with a close relative. Or maybe you will be able to avoid a crash on the way home because you had to turn back to get something you forgot.

We sometimes think we need to manage the Universe, but actually, the Universe is quite capable of managing itself perfectly.

So, where do you have resistance to let go of? Where are you stuck on controlling a specific situation? Can you let go of control? Can you surrender, even a little?

18.

....

WHAT WOULD WE DO IF WE HAD NO FEAR?

Fear is a normal part of everyday life. We carry fear with us wherever we go. But how much are we missing out on because of fear? What possibilities are we closed off to? What joyful experiences are we not pursuing?

Fear is insidious. It creeps into our thinking without our knowing. It blocks our dreams, hopes, and desires.

So how can we get unblocked? How can we recognize how fear is holding us back? By asking ourselves one simple question: *What would I do if I had no fear?*

It is amazing what that one question can evoke.

Keep in mind, I am not saying that you won't be afraid. Just that when we ask ourselves that question, a whole new world of possibilities suddenly emerges.

We may still be afraid. But once we know what we would do if we didn't feel fear, we can begin to move in that direction. We can bring the appropriate options to the table and act on them.

We do not have to eliminate our fear.

We do not have to work through our fear.

We just have to recognize where it is holding us back and move in that direction.

It is where we want to go. It is what we want to be doing anyway. We just didn't know it. Now we do. And now we also can take the smallest steps in that direction and bypass the fear.

So, what would you do, right now, if you had no fear? Can you see where your fear is holding you back?

PART TWO

OUR GROWTH

DISRUPTION, PROGRESS, AND FLOW

19.

....

THERE IS ALWAYS A PATH FORWARD

Sometimes we find ourselves in a bit of a mess. Everything around us seems to be exploding at the same time.

Too many things to do.

Too many places to be.

Too much on our plates.

And the stress of having to deal with it all builds up.

We become frustrated and scared. *Can I handle it all? How do I get it all done?* we wonder.

It does not matter if these are projects that we like or not. It does not matter if they are challenges that include other people or not. It is how we show up in the moment that makes all the difference. It is the knowing we embody that allows us to deal with it all.

Yet, what knowing is it that helps us feel less pressure and stress in that situation? It is the knowing that regardless of all the craziness we are experiencing, it is all already figured out and done on an energetic level. The knowing that as soon as we are faced with the challenges before us, the Universe has already created a path for their resolution. And that even when we can't figure things out for ourselves, the Universe has already figured it all out for us.

That our main job is just to be present. To take one step forward, or not. To put our energy into the one project that requires our attention at this moment, and know that through the interconnectedness of all things, that one step forward affects everything.

How do we know that the Universe has already created the path forward for us? By the sheer fact of what is before us. By the knowing that these projects or challenges would not have come to us if there was not a solution for moving forward. Even if the solution is to quit.

There is always a way forward. There is always a solution. There is always a single step we can take. We do not have to get it all done at once. We do not have to even see the ultimate solution to what we face in the moment. All we need to see is the next step.

The next few feet.

The path that stretches out before us.

Knowing that there is a solution, even if we can't see it, relieves the pressure. Allows us to take a breath. Brings us some internal peace. All so we can be more present and take that one small step. That one movement forward.

Sometimes the answer is to not move at all. To just wait and see what happens. It can take practice to find that quiet place inside. That is why meditation is so important, it helps us to find that quiet place when there is craziness all around us. And it is from that quiet place we feel when we pause that we can recognize when it is just time to wait.

There is always a myriad of things to do in our lives. Being at peace with that and knowing the Universe has already created a path forward, is the ultimate answer to finding that path. Life happens for us and is not done to us.

So where can you learn to be quiet and listen more? How can you take the time to just sit and wait to see what to go next?

20.

··

THE THREE MOST POWERFUL WORDS FOR GROWTH

Whenever we start to learn something new, it is hard to forget what we already know. We have accumulated so much knowledge over a lifetime that it is hard to see things that are new or to see familiar things from a different perspective. At these times, the three words *I don't know* can be immensely powerful words indeed.

To cultivate a beginner's mind, an attitude of openness and receptiveness, we can practice the phrase *I don't know*. To admit that we only know less than one billionth of what's out there, we can say, "*I don't know.*"

Sure, we may know a lot. Sure, what we are hearing may seem trite and boring. Yet we are different people than when we heard it before. Our experiences are different. Our perspectives are different. Our energy is different.

So even though we have heard the lesson before us a million times, embracing the mindset of *I don't know* can help us hear it in a new way. To see it in a new context. To accept it at a deeper level.

We can all use a little more humility. We can all use a beginner's mind to help us be more open, more flexible, more creative.

How many times have we said, "I know that," when, in fact, we didn't? How many times, even if we did know some great concept, didn't we put it into practice?

Sometimes, it's not about knowing it or understanding it.

It's about letting what we are being taught in to profoundly affect us.

To change us.

To surrender to what we are learning really has to teach us.

So where do you say *I know that* when there is something new for you to take in?

21.

....

CREATION IS ABOUT JOY AND THE POSSIBILITIES WITHIN US

We can all be creative. We create in different ways all the time and we don't have to be artists or musicians to be creative. So, what stops us from being creative? From feeling our creative juices flowing?

Is it about pressure and deadlines? Or about inspiration? Maybe we don't have enough free time to allow ourselves to play? Or maybe it is something else. . . . Maybe it has nothing to do with the external world. Maybe it has more to do with our connection to our soul.

Sometimes, when we feel that we've made a mistake or taken a wrong turn, we blame ourselves. We diminish and judge ourselves. When we do that, we cut ourselves off from our joy. From our passion. From our spirit.

When we feel unworthy or broken, how can we let new ideas in? How can we dance and play? It is only by connecting with our innocence that we can begin to create. To make something new. To solve a difficult problem or turn things around.

To connect to our innocence takes intimacy with ourselves. It takes truthfulness. It takes connection and community. For if we encourage ourselves just a little, we can achieve a lot.

If we can be gentle with ourselves and allow ourselves the time we need to heal our inner wounds, we can find that place inside of us, that place we hide away when we don't feel safe, that amazing little place where we feel whole and complete and can run wild.

There is joy inside, somewhere deep within all of us. Sometimes it surfaces. And then we allow ourselves to play, to create.

Creation is not about making something. It is about playing with our imagination. Freeing it to run wild in its field of possibilities. To conceive of what might be. Not what is.

Creation is about imbuing all the ideas before us with breath.

As you breathe and dance around in wonder and awe, what can you create today?

22.

....

TO GO WITH THE FLOW
REQUIRES REAL TRUST

To go with the flow is more difficult than we think. It takes more than just doing nothing. It takes more than just following the path in front of you. It is about true trust. It is about letting go of our expectations and allowing life to unfold unfettered.

We all have ideas and expectations of how we want things to go. We create plans and strategies for how to live our lives. And then life happens, and we learn to adjust those plans. Still, we work on trying to get where we want to go, even when the signs all point towards something else. We rush, we work harder, we work longer hours, we do whatever it takes to get it done.

The one thing we don't do is surrender to the moment. Let go of our expectations. Trust in life and in what unfolds before us. We think we know better. We think we are wiser than the circumstances before us.

What will it take for us to just breathe and trust the situation? What will it take for us to drop our ideas and our preconceptions? What will it take to release our judgments of what should and shouldn't be? When will we begin to see the Universe as being perfect, just the way it is?

When will we accept that we really don't have the perspective to judge the events before us as good or bad? Because when we finally do, then we can go with the flow

Then we can trust and allow.

Then we can be present to whatever is taking place and be at peace.

Is that not what we are all seeking?

Where can you trust more in your own life today?

23.

....

IT IS UP TO US TO LEARN THE LESSONS OF LIFE

Life will teach us new lessons every day if we are open to seeing and experiencing the lessons.

These lessons come to us in different ways. They can come from challenges. They can come from new relationships. They can come from misunderstandings.

Most of the time we create our own challenges. Through the choices we make. Through how we show up in the world.

We decide whether we will be difficult or easy with someone. We choose to drop our expectations, or not. We decide to open up or close down.

Life brings us to where we need to grow. It is our medicine. Then, it is up to us to take the medicine.

It is up to us to learn the lessons. It is our free will to decide to grow or stagnate. We all have the choice. We can choose to ignore the lessons in our lives or to embrace them.

Yes, it may not be easy to embrace the lessons. Yes, it can be painful to take a real, close look at ourselves. And yet, if we do, the reward is a more fulfilled life.

A more joyful life.

A more actualized life.

What lessons are in front you now? What is life calling you to learn or how is it calling you to grow?

24.

....

GROWTH HAPPENS IN THE DANCE BETWEEN FLUIDITY AND INTEGRITY

There is a dance we are all learning to do in our lives, a dance that life brings to us each day where we move from one extreme to the other. It is the dance between fluidity and integrity. The dance between keeping our word and dealing with crisis, between changing priorities and keeping the vision, between being present and remembering the goal.

Life brings us gifts in all sorts of ways. It challenges our sense of right and wrong. It makes us face our values and standards in unexpected ways. It tests our integrity.

In the dance of moving from being flexible to being true to our word, there is a vast space. A space we all learn to navigate over time. A space where we learn about what is profoundly important to us.

Do we worry about our image more than doing the *"right"* thing? Do we worry about what people will think of us? Are we concerned about the impact we have on other people?

What is most important to us always rises to the surface. And there we have an opportunity to truly examine ourselves. Our motivations and our struggles.

How do we adapt and change to any given situation? Are we hard on ourselves when we could not possibly live up to our word? Do we acknowledge it and hold ourselves accountable? Do we take actions to respond to what just happened?

Sometimes we have to break our own rules to uphold a higher purpose. To lend a hand to someone in need, or to stay present with someone who is going through a rough time. Sometimes we have to pull away from a loved one in order to fulfill other responsibilities.

Do we own it? All of it? How we show up when there are these kinds of challenges reveals much about who we are, and it is an opportunity for growth, self-reflection, and other kinds of inner work.

What kind of dance are you in?

How comfortable are you in movement from fluidity to integrity?

25.

WE ARE BOTH LIGHT AND DARK

To sit with our uncomfortable feelings is not easy. Our instinct is to avoid them and run away from them. No one wants to feel down, depressed, or anxious. Yet when we learn to navigate and hold these feelings, we can transform them.

We rarely have the intention to purposefully feel bad. We usually work towards feeling uplifted, joyful, and happy. Even so, it is important to remember that we are human beings. We have a wide range of emotions that run through our bodies. We are neither just light nor just dark, we are all the colors of the rainbow and more.

Life is not just about living during the daytime; it is also about living during the night. To walk around during the day is easy. We can see all the obstacles in our path and avoid them.

Walking at night is more difficult. Without the light, it is harder to see what is in front of us. We learn to adjust our eyes to open wider to take in what little data there is.

To learn to walk in the darkness is valuable indeed.

To learn to move forward in our lives when we feel dark is just as valuable.

As we become more comfortable being able to walk through our lives when we don't feel like walking at all, our comfort will serve us tremendously. For we are meant to grow and learn. We are meant to stand up for ourselves. We are meant to show our strength even when we don't feel strong. A deeper strength often arises from our adversity.

It is connection to our inner light that holds us up when otherwise we would fall down. And it is in the integration of all that we are—darkness included—that we find our true selves.

We are both light and dark, both happy and sad, both joyful and blue.

How comfortable are you with your darkness? Where do you need practice walking in your life?

26.

....

SLOWING DOWN MAY BE THE FASTEST WAY TO GET WHERE WE'RE GOING

You see it everywhere. People are rushing from one place to the next. Rushing to get their projects done. Rushing to go home, go away, go get their coffee.

We rush because we think that's the fastest way to get something done, yet when we rush all the time, we miss things. We miss the little details that make all the difference. We miss the birds chirping as we walk to the train. We miss the error in the program as we rush to finish the app. We miss the look on our partner's face as we rush out the door to get to work.

Sometimes, perhaps even most times, by slowing down we actually are going the fastest way. By slowing down, we can take in more. By slowing down, we can be more present. By slowing down, we can feel more of what is going on inside and outside of us.

When we take the time to really look at what is going on, either at work, at home, or anywhere in between, we can often find a better, simpler, more direct way to achieve what we are looking for.

This idea may be counterintuitive, yet it still works. Even taking the time to ask, *What am I trying to achieve?* can slow us down and help to remind us what it is we are really after.

Did we slow down enough to read the entire article? Did we slow down enough to see the smile on our lover's lips? Did we slow down enough to see the potential hazard on the road?

Speed does not equal the shortest distance. Taking our time is sometimes the fastest way to get where we are going. Or perhaps it is just about recognizing that we are already there.

Where in your life can you slow down to speed up?

27.

....

CHAOS ALLOWS US TO GO FROM EVOLUTIONARY TO REVOLUTIONARY

Human beings usually do not like to deal with or allow chaos. We like things orderly and neat, everything in its place. It makes for a more efficient workplace, and a less stressful home environment.

Yet, when we allow things to go a little crazy, when we allow some chaos into our orderly lives, it can bring tremendous transformation and change.

In an orderly environment, change happens slowly, if at all, and in tiny, incremental steps. When we blow things up, create a mess, spread it out all over the place, then revolutionary new patterns can emerge. Then we can take a completely new and fresh perspective on issues we've been dealing with for years.

The mess gives us an opportunity to come up that next great idea, that new relationship, that amazing insight.

Evolutionary growth is fine.

Revolutionary leaps forward are rare and amazing!

So, where can you create a revolutionary mess in your life? One that truly serves you?

28.

....

PROGRESS IS HIDDEN BY HOW CLOSE WE ARE TO IT

When we look at ourselves in the mirror each day, it is easy to miss the changes in our appearance. Our daily progress in acquiring skills and making progress in our lives, our careers, and our businesses is just as easy to miss because it often is incremental and slow, barely noticeable. It is only by taking a step back that we can see how far we have come. Or anyone else, for that matter.

The people closest to us are usually the last people to notice what's different. Like letting go of those extra couple of pounds or getting into shape. It is only when we meet someone who has not seen us for a while that we get real feedback. How different we look is much more evident to them because of the time that has passed since they last saw us.

Perspective gives us much more contrast to work with. How things used to be to how things are now is so much clearer. Even to ourselves.

Before getting upset at others for not noticing changes in us, we must ask ourselves, *Do I see the change in them?*

Usually not.

We are all guilty of it. Not because we don't want to see changes, but because we are just too close. It's like a pointillist painting that up close only looks like a bunch of dots, yet when we step back and get further away from the painting, patterns begin to emerge. If we step even further back, the new perspective reveals the true picture.

This is so true of life as well. When we are too close to the source, we cannot see the pattern. We cannot see how things are different. Then, as we step back and allow time to give us a new perspective, the change emerges into our view.

It was always there. Yet without the new perspective, we could not see it.

So how much distance do you need to see changes in yourself? How long does it take you to see the growth and transformation that is taking place right before your eyes? Could you step back today and measure your progress?

29.

························

IF WE RECOGNIZE OUR PROGRESS, WE DON'T NEED ANOTHER'S PRAISE

"That's nice, but you can do better."

How often do we hear words that don't really acknowledge us? The person thinks they are being supportive. They think they are helping us to do better. Yet that lack of true recognition only brings us down.

It is not so uncommon that we feel we've done something good, either at home, at work, or for some organization. We feel good about what we've accomplished. We feel we have improved and reached a higher level of achievement, and in our joy and excitement we ask for someone else's opinion. But when they give it, we wish we hadn't—for as soon as the words they say leave their lips, we know we are in for disappointment.

We can feel the criticism coming with the first syllable. *"You can do better."*

Of course, we can. And we will. Really all we wanted was for them to say, "Good job," and mean it.

We all feel a need validation for from someone else at some point. We all crave some words of encouragement. But all too often we are met with a cold, uncaring comment.

That insensitive comment bites hard. And when we remember that sting, it helps us to think about what we say to others. How do they feel when we criticize them? They are no different than us. And we can all do better at showing our support and encouragement. We can all be kinder and gentler to other people.

Most of all, we can be kinder and gentler to ourselves. If the world around us does not recognize our achievements, we can recognize them ourselves. We can go out and celebrate by ourselves or with someone else who is supportive and caring. We do not have to seek recognition from someone who is unwilling or unable to give it. We can find another way to feel good about ourselves.

Looking for recognition externally is a trap, because often the validation of effort and intention we seek simply does not come. If we can learn to self-validate our efforts, then the lack of recognition from others does not sting as much. The charge around it is lessened.

And sometimes it is just about choice. Perhaps the person we are looking for recognition from is just not someone who can give it. Perhaps they never received it themselves, so they do not know how to give it.

So, let's look elsewhere. Let's find someone who is capable of giving it. Let's ask someone whom we know actually wants to encourage us.

Sometimes the best choice we can make is to just keep quiet and smile to ourselves. And sometimes it is just about asking a different person.

Who in your life can you count on to celebrate with you? What kind of self-recognition can you give yourself?

30.

·······································

PAIN IS A MESSAGE ABOUT NEEDING TO CHANGE

Pain is a great communicator. You cannot ignore it or avoid it.

We may spend a great deal of time attempting to make it go away instead of listening to it, but pain always has a message to it. It is here to inform us that something needs to change.

It does not matter whether it is physical pain or emotional pain, the message is the same: Something is not working properly, and we need to look at it. Something is stuck, and we need to release it. Something is misaligned, and we need to balance it.

Often, we judge pain as bad, and that makes it all the more painful. If we can release our judgment of pain and pay attention to it instead of rejecting it, we have taken the first step to releasing it. Listening to the pain, really delving into it and being open to its message, is the surest way to get past it.

As long as we stuff it down, ignore it, and avoid it at all costs, it will persist. It will continue and we'll miss a great opportunity to learn.

Where is your pain? What is it telling you? How can you be more open to it?

31.

·····················

WE ALL HAVE DOG DAYS EVERY NOW AND THEN

We all have dog days every now and then, times when we feel like the world is against us. We all wake up on the wrong side of the bed once in a while.

The key to surviving such days is not to marinate in the misery but to accept that they're tough.

Feeling awful? Great! Feel it!

Let's not stuff down the uncomfortable feelings. Let's not ignore the signs that are telling us it's time to take a break. Let's not forget that will always be ups and downs.

If we can stop judging the downs as bad, we can get through them with greater ease. When we truly accept all that life brings to us, regardless of how good or bad it feels, somehow things just go smoother.

It's okay to have a dog day, just don't drag it around with you for the rest of your life.

So where are you not feeling so great? How can you accept that uncomfortable feeling and move forward?

32.

....

BEING TRIGGERED IS ALWAYS ABOUT US

When we allow others to be who they are without having to change them or get them to believe what we believe, we actually give ourselves more freedom to be who we are. What calls to us to change in others is merely a reflection of what we desire to change within ourselves.

It might not seem directly applicable, yet in some way the very things that annoy and irk us about someone else, things that cause us to cringe when we think about this other person, are the very same things hidden in the dark corners of our psyche that we feel are untenable.

We usually think it's all about the other person when we react badly to someone. It's not. It's actually always about us. If we didn't have an irritating thorn in our own side that causes us pain when someone else reflects it back to us, then those traits would not annoy us at all. It is only because those characteristics hit home and ring true within us that we have a reaction at all.

No, it's not about them. Yes, it is always about us. Maybe not directly, maybe not in the same way or about the thing, yet it is there, somewhere, lurking in the recesses of our mind.

Now that you know that, don't you feel a bit more compassion for others?

33.

....

PLAY CAN BE DEEP WORK

Sometimes, play can be deep inner work.

Yes, it can be superficial. Yes, it can be just a distraction. Yes, it can be nothing but play. But it also can be just what we need.

Play is how the mind makes new connections. Play is how we learn and grow. When we get too serious, too stressed, we need play more than ever.

When we want to be more creative, play is necessary. When we want to find a new solution, play allows us to be free.

Making time to play is never a waste. The results may not show up right away, yet they will follow. Perhaps we should all play a little more often and learn to be playful when doing our most serious work.

Are you taking enough time to play in your life?

34.

....

BALANCE HAPPENS OVER AN ENTIRE LIFE, NOT IN A DAY, OR A WEEK

Work-life balance is something rarely achieved. We think that's what we want to have in life, yet we actually need to be uneven in our focus to operate well in this world. Sometimes, we need to work more. Other times, we need to focus on our relationships. Still other times, we need to pay more attention to our health. Life does not often give us a chance to do all this and more on the same day.

When we are young, our health is usually strong, and we desire to build our career or business. As we mature, finding a partner and creating a family becomes important to us. Then, as we age and get on in years, our health is of primary concern.

There is nothing wrong with having different priorities at different times. We do not need to be perfectly balanced and focusing on all things at all times. Perhaps one week we want to spend more time connecting with friends. The next week we desire to be more with our family or parents. Still at other times we are working hard to get a project done. Or perhaps we are spending a great deal of time looking for a new job or switching careers. Maybe even going back to school to learn a new skill or technology. Sometimes, we even come down with wanderlust and decide to spend our days traveling the world. Focusing intensely on one of these areas more than the others is not only normal but expected.

And when the time comes that we decide to spend as much time as possible with a dying relative or a friend with a serious disease, that is appropriate too.

The balance in life is not about what area we are focusing our daily schedule on. It is about having a full, well-rounded life that we will look back upon one day and feel satisfied. Balance occurs most often in the long view of life, not in the short term.

So, let's stop criticizing ourselves for not having more balance in our lives, and start accepting that it is all just a part of life.

Where in your life do you need to be a little out of balance?

What requires your attention more today than yesterday?

35

OUR MISTAKES ARE NOT HERE TO MAKE US FEEL BAD, THEY ARE HERE TO TEACH US

Sometimes we feel powerless to do anything about our circumstances, possibly because they are the result of what we have done in the past. Or possibly because the forces involved are so much greater than us.

Yet our personal power is not about changing others. It is about changing ourselves.

Yes, we make mistakes. Yes, sometimes we do things that we know are not in complete alignment. Yes, sometimes we do take a shortcut and then it blows up in our face.

Now, we are forced to deal with the consequences of our actions. Those things that we thought no one would ever find out. The things we were so careful to keep hidden.

Now they all come out.

And there is nothing we can do about it, except admit to what we have done and take responsibility for it. Even if there was not a malicious intent this is the right thing to do.

We may be powerless to stop the forces at work, yet if we learn our lesson and stand up for what's right and accept the results of the seeds we have sown, then we can move forward.

We cannot change the past or what we have already done. We cannot un-ring that bell. So, to find our sense of balance and power, we must accept.

Accept what has happened.

Accept what we have caused, intentional or not.

Accept that it is now our turn to own up to our mistakes.

We can learn to be better for it. We can come to a new place of transparency and honesty. We can move forward not to get past it, not to get through it, but to own it.

Yes, we may lick our wounds and bow our heads in shame. Yet we cannot stay in shame. So, we pick ourselves up, look for the support we need, and begin again. As if for the first time. Learning to be better for what we experienced.

Yes, it hurts. Yet we don't have to live there. And with time, we can raise our heads once again to see the sunshine.

So, what mistakes have you made that you learned a lot from? What mistakes are you ready to forgive yourself for?

36.

··

WHEN RESISTANCE APPEARS, IT JUST MEANS THERE IS A BETTER WAY

When we face challenges in our lives, most people have a tendency to push through a problem. We effort and grit our teeth as we work incredibly hard to get where we want to go. Yet how often do we stop and think about whether there is a better way?

In today's world, it's all about strength of will and sheer determination. It's about *crushing it*, *pounding on the desk*, and sheer *force*. We rarely stop to think about the consequences of such an attitude, especially the cost on our health. These approaches reveal an underlying belief that life doesn't really support us.

What if, instead of having to *kill ourselves* to get something accomplished, we were able to allow something to blossom?

What if life really does support us when we are in alignment, and we learned to accept how things worked out?

Imagine if you can, what your life would be like if instead of every place where you found you had to exert extreme force, you merely took a step back and tried a different way? How much more could we achieve if we listened to life and paid attention to where there wasn't resistance? It all comes down to our beliefs. Do we believe life is constantly guiding us or that we have to go it alone? Do we believe life wants us to succeed and spread more good things in the world, or is it totally indifferent?

When we choose to believe that life is supporting us, constantly and always, the life we lead becomes one of less struggle, not more. Accomplishment becomes something we receive, instead of something we must work hard at.

Which world would you rather live in?

PART THREE

OUR WILL

ENERGY, INTEGRITY, AND
EMPOWERMENT

....

37

TRUSTING OURSELVES IS WHERE ALL EMPOWERMENT BEGINS

Trusting ourselves is one of the greatest challenges, especially if we are conscientious. Because we know all the things we have done wrong in the past, because we are acutely aware of all of our impure motivations, and because we are keenly sensitive to all the harsh judgments we have witnessed our whole lives, trust in oneself may be hard to come by.

Can we trust ourselves enough not to second-guess our choices? Can we trust ourselves enough to know that our intentions are good, if not pure?

Can we trust ourselves enough to believe in our dreams even when no one else does? Can we trust ourselves enough to keep going when everything seems to be against us?

Trust is built slowly, one baby step at a time. First, let's start with trusting ourselves that we are showing up the best that we can. Then, let's trust ourselves to walk the path in front of us, first slowly, then trusting we can pick up the pace.

Then, how about we learn to trust not only our choices and our decisions, but our ideas, our connections, and our leadership as well?

We can build trust in ourselves, if we are willing to start small, count every little victory, and then keep our focus on all the things we do right.

Repeat after me, "I trust myself!"

38.

··

HARMONY IS WHEN WE FLOW EFFORTLESSLY FROM BEING TO DOING

Sometimes we focus too much on doing—especially in the western world, where productivity is so highly regarded. To find balance, we then must focus on being.

Both doing and being have a place in our lives. Both are important. They're like two sides of the same coin.

When we learn to be more of who we are, we can do from a deeper place. When we take the time to meditate on what it is we want to be, what we want to do becomes more obvious. Yet when we spend too time on the doing, we get too busy to just be.

Yes, we create a lot of things when we focus on the doing. We build everything from bridges to social media followings. We write books, close deals, and create new organizations.

Yet, doing can become a trap. We can get hooked on pursuing the next goal, the next accomplishment, the next thing to do.

It is only when we take a step back to just breath that we can see things a little more clearly. When we allow ourselves to take a break and just be.

Be in nature.

Be with friends and family.

Or just be alone.

We can then ask ourselves why we are doing all the things we do. We can then look at if it is all in alignment with what we are about. Is our doing fully embodying our being? Is what we are creating truly an expression of what our essence calls us to?

At the same time, if all we do is focus on how to be, then do we really accomplish anything? Are we bringing some creation into the world from our being?

Harmony is achieved when we learn to flow effortlessly from being to doing and from doing to being.

It takes time to master this flow, yet isn't it worth it?

39.

....

WE CREATE OUR LIVES THROUGH OUR FOCUS, ENERGY, AND DECISIONS

Taking responsibility for our lives is not easy. It means accepting that we create all the good stuff and all the bad stuff in our lives. It means there is no one else to blame for our situation. Yet it also means we are empowered to create something different.

Often, we fall into the trap of making excuses and blaming others for where we are in life—blaming our parents, our teachers, our coaches, our bosses, or our lovers. We may feel sad or angry or upset because of what someone else has done. Or think we cannot do what we truly want because of our responsibilities to others. Yet, who agreed to be in those situations to begin with? We did.

How we came to our choices and decisions may go far back. Perhaps a decision we made in school had far-reaching effects on our life. At the time, we had no clue how that one little choice would send us in a totally different trajectory. Then, step by step, we moved toward one thing or away from another. Until we arrived here.

The energy we put into each situation has consequences and moves us further towards or away from what we want. As days and weeks and months pass, we may forget our original choices. Years go by and instead of being in one place we are in a completely different place.

So, who is to say that it's better or worse than someplace else? Ultimately all that we know is that it is a place of our own making. It is a place formulated by our own choices. It is a situation that arises from the energy we have put out, which means we are responsible for where we are and what to do next about it.

Yes, that means we have to take credit for all the bad as well as all the good around us.

Yes, that means we have created our lives to be exactly how they are at this moment.

The good news is that we can always learn to make different choices. As long as we are still breathing, we have an opportunity to do something different. The real question is what we are going to do with this power.

What are you going to create next in your life?

Where are you going to focus your energy? What new decisions are you going to make?

40.

....

INTEGRITY CREATES INFLUENCE—AND INFLUENCE IS GOLDEN

Integrity is not just about showing up. Integrity is much more encompassing. It includes our words, our deeds, our actions, and our intentions.

First, we can build trust by showing up consistently. Then, we can build trust by living up to our words. That's when people look at our deeds and actions to see if they are in alignment with the things we say.

Sure, it is easy to find people who say one thing and do something else. Many of them get away with it for quite a long time. Eventually though, the inconsistent nature of their actions is revealed, and people stop believing them.

They may never say a word or give any feedback. The lack of integrity turns them away and they feel no compunction to let the person know.

Yet a beautiful thing happens when our words and actions are aligned on a consistent basis. People start to trust us on a very deep level. That level of trust gives us real influence, and that influence must be treated as the most precious gift. For it is. It is more precious than gold for that influence allows us to share our work and ourselves to an enthusiastic community.

That community is what will support us for the rest of our days.

Where has integrity created more influence for you? In your work? With your family, your friends? Do you cherish the influence that your integrity has given you?

41.

....

LIVING UP TO OUR COMMITMENTS IS ABOUT MORE THAN KEEPING OUR WORD

Commitment is about much more than just making a decision.

Yes, it starts with a decision, a decision that has been weighed carefully, outcomes considered, and the responsibilities that go with the commitment. Unfortunately, we are not always the best predicators of what's involved. All too often we commit to something without truly considering the full implications. Once the full consequences of the commitment are revealed, we may then retreat and may even end up breaking our commitment.

When we start taking our commitments more seriously, treating them as something sacred, we may not get into them so easily, and when we do commit, our word is our bond and we fully live up to it.

If we find we are having a hard time living up to all of our commitments, then it is time to examine how we enter into our commitments, and whether we are truly reflecting on what it means to make a commitment in the first place.

We can all do better around our commitments if we just take our time before entering them, really reflect upon them, and only commit when we are confident it is in alignment with our heart and our spirit.

How do you enter into commitments? Have you ever taken time to examine how seriously you take those commitments? Is your word your bond?

42.

························

OUR STRONGEST MOMENTS HAPPEN WHEN WE ARE MOST VULNERABLE

Connection is something we all long for. Even with our own family. Even with our own community. Yet connection only happens when there is vulnerability.

Are we vulnerable enough to tell our friend that we are going through a rough time? Are we vulnerable enough to tell our brother or sister about the trauma we experienced as a child that they never knew about? Are we vulnerable enough to tell those around us that we are not sure what to do next?

We think we have to keep an air of *I've got it all together* in order for our friends to think we're okay. We think if we show the world we are hurting it will only punish us more.

Actually, the world can relate to us more if we share our struggles and our pain. The more human we make ourselves the more comfortable people feel around us. The more honest we are about what is really going on inside us the closer our partners will feel to us. To only show one side of ourselves to others creates a one-dimensional image of who we are.

We are so much more complex and intricate. We are full of contradictions and paradoxes. And if we allow ourselves to show that to the world at large, or just to our best friend, then we can create a deeper connection.

To say to your boss or your clients that you don't know how to handle something is brave. As long as it is followed by a request for help to find out what to do next, they will reward our bravery.

If we don't express ourselves because of fear, we may hurt ourselves. We may hurt our reputation and trustworthiness in their eyes. To be trustworthy, we must be honest and vulnerable with them. For others to feel that we are safe, we must be honest about what is really going on.

Sometimes even we ourselves don't know what is going on inside of us. When this happens, we can be honest about that as well.

Being vulnerable may seem as if we are being weak, but nothing is further from the truth. Our strongest moments happen when we are being the most vulnerable.

Is there a place in your life that being more vulnerable will serve you? Can you open up and be honest about something that is scary to share with someone you trust?

43.

....

RESPECTING OURSELVES IS THE FIRST STEP TO RECEIVING RESPECT

It is easy to get confused as to why other people don't respect us. We are nice to them. We bend over backwards for them. Yet they still treat us with disrespect and callousness.

It just doesn't add up.

Why would they do such a thing? It is a paradox. Sometimes it just seems that the nicer we are to others, the less they appreciate it.

In this paradox is a message from the Universe: It is not about being nice. It is about respect. We must first learn to respect ourselves before others will start respecting us.

How do we do that? By respecting our time, our effort, and our energy. By creating and communicating clear boundaries for ourselves and sticking to them.

When we allow other to cross our boundaries, it often does not work out well, for when people see there are no consequences for not considering our boundaries, they will continue to push. They may push and push and push until we finally say, *"No more!"*

When we start to truly respect ourselves, we hold fast to our boundaries. When we respect our time and energy, we make sure people know there are consequences. When we truly demonstrate self-respect, we are signaling the Universe that we only wish to deal with people who respect us as well.

The key to receiving respect from others?

Respecting ourselves, pure and simple.

Can you see where you can have more respect for yourself? Stronger boundaries with others?

44.

························

STANDING UP FOR OURSELVES IS NOT SELFISH, IT IS HOW WE MEET OUR NEEDS

For some of us, the lesson of standing up for ourselves is a big one. We have been taught to be nice and not cause trouble. We give in too easily to others' demands or we do not ask for what we want or need.

There is a better way to show up. We can stand up for ourselves without being belligerent. We can stand up for ourselves and ask for what we need without getting emotional. We can stand up for ourselves by simply saying no.

Standing up for ourselves does not mean we are being selfish. It does not mean we are self-centered. It only means that we value ourselves and our needs.

If we all learned to stand up for ourselves in a firm yet gentle manner, life would be clearer. Boundaries would be more evident. Desires would be more out in the open.

When our desires do not match what the other is willing or able to give, we can walk away without any hard feelings. Expectations would be clear from the start. Our positions at work and at home would be apparent. And because all of these things would be more recognizable, we would actually receive more of what we need.

What kind of world would we be living in if that were the case?

Where can you be standing up for yourself more in your life? Where can you make your yeses and your nos clearer?

45.

....

THE KINDER WE ARE WITH OURSELVES, THE EASIER IT IS TO TAKE RESPONSIBILITY

How do we take responsibility for our actions? How do we show up when we've made a mistake or done something we thought better of afterward? Do we justify and throw blame on to others, or do we go beyond the idea of blame and merely make right what we have done?

All too often in this society, we find that people fear to take responsibility for their actions and words. We see how people deny or change what happened out of fear.

Fear drives us to hide from the consequences of our deeds. We fear how others will respond and react to what we have said or done. We fear it not because of what others may do but because of our own judgments about ourselves. We fear it because we are being too hard on ourselves, and secretly we are condemning ourselves long before anyone else knows what happened. This is because we are always our own worst critic, our own worst detractor.

We are far harsher on ourselves than anyone else can ever be.

Our fears are not about what others may do. Our fears are about merely being exposed and being seen for what we have done. We fear being human. We fear making mistakes.

Yet when we allow ourselves to be human and make mistakes, we allow others to do the same. When we become more compassionate toward ourselves, we can be more compassionate toward others.

And when we all soften into compassion for being human, there is no reason to be afraid to take responsibility.

We are all guilty of something, so let's be more kind to ourselves and to everyone else.

Is there something in your life you can now take responsibility for? Can you clean it up and make it right without making yourself wrong?

46.

···

FORGIVING OURSELVES IS THE KEY TO EMBODYING INTEGRITY

We all have ideas of how we are supposed to be. We talk about them to others whenever we have a chance. We believe in them and we help others with them. Yet how often do we find that we don't follow these ideas ourselves?

It's human, of course. We don't always walk the talk.

That's okay. As long as we reflect on the times we don't. Look at why we didn't practice what we preach. Perhaps it was just an isolated incident. Or is it part of a larger pattern?

How often do we not listen to our own advice? Is it a once in while occurrence or something more regular? Maybe there is something in that particular instance that is a trigger?

Is there a clue in there about something deeper? Maybe a childhood trauma? Maybe something more recent?

We all have triggers and traumas. That's normal and human. Yet the more we can be aware of them, the less they control us.

Self-reflection and Self-examination are the keys to growth. When we step out of integrity it is a sign to look at ourselves.

As we live our life in the real world, we often strive to become more in integrity. Beating ourselves up along the way does not help. Yes, we need to own it when we fall out of integrity and at the same time we can all learn to be gentler with ourselves when it does happen.

Forgiveness is not just for others. It is also for ourselves. The more we forgive ourselves, the more we can learn to embody the integrity we may feel we have lost.

Where have you fallen out of integrity? Can you forgive yourself for it? Can you clean it up and move forward and accept that you are human?

47.

....

BEING HONEST WITH OURSELVES ABOUT REALITY IS HOW WE EMPOWER OURSELVES

We all see life as we want it to be. Sometimes, that is how it is. Many times, it is not.

Our vision of what is going on is often clouded by our desires. This is what causes us to not see the reality of life.

Perhaps we want things to work out so badly that we ignore the warning signs in a relationship. Maybe we are so invested in our business we don't see the change in the market. Sometimes we ignore warning signs of poor health, not wanting to believe that we could be sick. This difference between our perception and reality is an important one to recognize.

How do we become more in alignment with reality?

It is about understanding ourselves and our desires. It is about knowing ourselves well enough to see our own biases.

It is about being honest enough with ourselves that we want something so badly we could not be seeing clearly.

This is not easy to do. It takes real courage to see life as it really is. The level of honesty about our own hopes, dreams, and desires must be high.

It is easy to kid ourselves. It is easy to believe we really are seeing things accurately. It takes work to question ourselves and be willing to be open to receiving the answer we don't want.

None of us wants to hear that things are not as we desire. None of us intentionally wants to know that things are worse than we think. Yet, if we allow ourselves to be so brutally honest with ourselves, then we are empowered to do something about it. Then we can take the appropriate action. Then we can be prepared for what is to come, even if it is unpleasant.

It is better to see life as it really is than to be surprised by what was in front of us the entire time.

So, where have you been kidding yourself? Where can you be a little more honest with yourself about what is going so that you can take the next appropriate step? Be gentle with yourself around it but be honest.

48.

....

AS WE ACCEPT ALL OF OURSELVES, BALANCE GIVES WAY TO HARMONY

We often think of being balanced as the goal—usually we are interested in attaining the balance of two opposite and complementary aspects of our personalities, like the part that wants to sleep late and the part that wants to be an early riser. Or we strive to balance the many aspects of our lives, such as career and home life.

Yet a permanent state of balance is unrealistic, so perhaps a better word to use is *harmony.* For even if we can achieve balance in our lives, it is always short lived.

How can we sustain balance in our relationships, our work, our health, our finances, and our growth all at the same time? When we concentrate on one area of life it is usually at the expense of another. If we focus on our career or finances, perhaps our relationships or health will suffer.

Sometimes if we look to balance the energy within us, we do ourselves a disservice. For if we show up with our feminine and masculine traits in balance for a football game, we are not likely to do well. If we show up with aggressive and passive energies completely balanced for a date, we may not be able to make that heart-to-heart connection we so desire.

Balance is overrated. It is an ideal that is not sustainable, and it does not serve us well in our lives.

Sometimes we need to go to extremes. Sometimes we need to be imbalanced to meet a given situation properly. So we work on the dance between opposites.

We learn how to be more fluid.

And as we become better and better at accepting and using all of our aspects, we become more of who we are.

We are light and dark.

We are strong and weak.

We are masculine and feminine.

We are courageous and scared.

We are connected and alone.

We are passionate and passive.

We are joyful and depressed.

We are driven and apathetic.

We are caring and insensitive.

For we are all these things and more, and as we learn to flow from one to another, we learn what works best in any given moment.

Balance gives way to harmony, and in harmony we are more fully who we are meant to be.

So, where are you trying to be balanced in your life that perhaps you should seek harmony instead? Where can you be more fluid and less rigid in your thinking that can serve you in the moment and in your life?

....

49

ALL OUR PREPARATION IS FOR THE MOMENT WE HAVEN'T PREPARED FOR

We prepare for all sorts of things.

We prepare the best we can.

We practice, rehearse, and go over things again and again.

And then the day comes when we have to let it all go because we've prepared enough. We've memorized all we can. We've done the best we can to be ready for that moment.

Whether it is for a speech, a book launch, an interview, or a presentation. It does not matter what we have prepared for, it is all the same. When that moment comes when we must step forward and perform, it is time to be present. To listen to that voice inside us that tells us exactly what to do. To be in the moment and drop all the rules, all the formulas, and really be with what is in front of us.

It is time to be fluid. For all the plans in the world could not have prepared us for this moment. This moment when things don't go according to plan. This moment when things don't work the way we expect. This moment when suddenly we have to deal with something we have never thought of—this black swan event.

That's when all the preparation kicks in, not to tell us exactly what to do. But to give us the confidence to figure out what to do when we never thought of this moment.

Now is the time our intuition kicks in. Now is the time we step into action before we have a chance to think about it. Now is the time our body moves without our thought because it has been preparing for this moment for so long.

We don't have to be perfect. Indeed, we live in an imperfect world, so nothing is ever perfect. Yet we can respond to the situation the best we can because we have prepared for everything else.

Now we perform—because that is what we are designed to do. That is what we want to do. That is what has motivated us from the beginning.

And regardless of what happens, it will be perfect because we will learn and grow from it. And we will be even more prepared for the next time.

Where in your life have you prepared enough? Where can you just show up and allow all the preparation you've done to serve you? And where do you need to prepare some more?

....

50

BRINGING JOY TO OUR CHALLENGES IS HOW WE GLIDE THROUGH THEM

Challenges are not something we need to avoid. Although they are not comfortable, they do serve a purpose. They push us beyond what we thought our limits are. They help us to get out of our comfort zone and bring real growth.

Just like an animal that must shed its skin to grow, the process is uncomfortable. Just like a seed that must exert immense pressure to break through its case, it's not easy. Yet in order for our muscles to grow strong, they need resistance to push against.

In order for us to build our emotional, physical and spiritual muscles, we must push against resistance. Once we have developed our muscles, then we can dance with it. After we have gone through our transformation, then we can use our new wings and fly.

When we are in the middle of our challenges, they don't feel very nice. Yes, when we are experiencing the very things we want to avoid, we don't feel good. If we judge our experiences and make them wrong or bad, we are only making it more difficult for ourselves. But if we can face the challenge without judgment and criticism, we may find it a little easier to get through.

When we release our expectations and let go of our opinions about the challenges we face, then we can allow them to unfold more naturally and more quickly. And in the end, is that not what we truly want? To get through our challenges as quickly as possible?

It is up to us to stop resisting our difficulties. The choice and the power to overcome them is within us. We can choose to fight against them and try to push them away, or we can embrace them.

In fact, we could go even further and revel in them. We could bring our joy to the entire process and then see what happens.

Do you have a challenge you are experiencing that you can bring more joy to? Is there a challenge you have been resisting that you can embrace and accept to make it easier to face?

51.

....

SHIFTING FROM BLAME TO CHOICE EMPOWERS US BEYOND MEASURE

Our personal power starts to end the moment we begin to blame someone or something else. It does not matter what they did, or what happened to us, it only matters that we allow the circumstance to dictate our reaction.

Our power comes from our presence and our ability to decide how we choose to respond to any given situation. Blaming and making either someone else or the situation wrong, merely takes away our ability to move past it. When we decide how we want to be in the situation regardless of the truth of it, then we are exercising our most important muscle. It is the muscle of choice. It is the muscle of our spirit. It is the muscle of our divine right to create our life anew.

Resisting what is only causes us pain and keeps us stuck where we are.

To acknowledge the truth of the reality of the situation, yet not allow the truth to dictate our behavior is the surest way to build our personal power.

Being present to a situation that is unpleasant is a choice. Being present with compassion and love for ourselves is one of the greatest choices we can ever make. So, let's stop resisting the reality, let's stop blaming anyone or anything else, and let's focus on what we can do instead.

When we shift from blame to choice we empower ourselves beyond measure.

Where in your life are you blaming someone else? Where can you shift from blame to choice?

52.

....

IF WE TAKE RESPONSIBILITY FOR OUR PART, WE CAN CHANGE OUR LIFE

There is one magical key for changing our life, one ingredient that we have to include to evolve.

It is not about a secret practice or ritual. It is simply this: We have to take responsibility for our part in life. We have to take responsibility for how we show up in the world. We have to take responsibility for our side of the relationship.

This does not mean we have to take responsibility for anyone else's part. Only our own part. Others have to have to take responsibility for their part. And that is their work, not ours.

Our work is to truly take responsibility, so we are empowered to change. For it is only when we truly take responsibility that we recognize our power. That we see how we are a creator. That we know we have contributed to everything in our lives.

We are not responsible for what happens to us. We are responsible for how we react to it. For the meaning we make from it. And for the next choice we make.

We cannot change the past. Yet we can change the present moment. By making a different choice. By own our past participation. By accepting that we can be different.

We can change. We can choose a different path. And then we can move forward. Consciously, with intention and awareness.

How others decide to respond to us is their business. Ours is to own our part and move forward with intention. That's how we change our life.

Is there somewhere in your life you want to take responsibility for how you reacted? Can you shift your reaction to one that is more conscious, more aware?

53.

....

PRESSURE CAN SERVE US IF WE VIEW IT AS SOMETHING THAT SUPPORTS US

Pressure is a funny thing. It can make us stronger, like a diamond. Or it can break us down, like broken glass. The key to getting stronger is time and perspective.

If we are put under pressure for an extended period of time we will break. Yet shorter exposure to pressure actually helps us to grow.

And a great deal of what happens to us has to do with our internal story. Is this a bad thing happening to us? Or is it a necessary force to help us achieve something?

We all respond to pressure differently. We all have different stories around pressure. Some people thrive under pressure. Some people just cave in and collapse. When we can examine what our pressure story is, we can better deal with it.

A lot of it also has to do with our basic operating system.

Do we believe life is out to get us? Do we believe life is here for us? Do we believe things always work out for us? Do we believe we never get a break? All of these hidden thought patterns affect how we respond to the normal pressures of life.

They also dictate how we respond to the extraordinary pressure of an unexpected event. Do we take it as an opportunity to grow? Or do we view it as another annoyance?

How we bring ourselves into the situation is key. Are we curious and excited? Do we have foreboding and dread? Pressure pushes us forward in many ways, as long as we feel the pressure is not out to destroy us.

We all have pressure in our lives. We can't escape it. Yet we can learn to view it in ways that support us. It is all up to us. Change the story around pressure and you will change your life.

Are you feeling pressure that is stopping you from being your best? Can you reframe that pressure into something that is supporting you?

54.

....

STANDING UP FOR THE RIGHT THING CAN FEEL LONELY UNTIL WE SEE THE IMPACT

Sometimes, when we stand up for what we believe in, we get knocked down. We get stabbed in the back for having a conscience. We get ridiculed for opening our mouth and speaking our truth. And it feels like the entire world is turning against us.

Society doesn't like when we rock the boat, especially when we have higher standards than most. The crowd doesn't appreciate it when we call out one of their own.

It can feel very lonely to make a stand, yet we do it anyway. We do it because in our heart we know it is the right thing to do. We don't do it to be popular. We don't do it to win favors. We do it because we have to, because of who we are even if it appears no one appreciates it. We can't hold our tongue. We feel we must speak up and say what we see.

It can feel discouraging to be the only one to make a stand. The response can make us feel like we should not have cared so much. And we may start to question whether we should have spoken up at all. Perhaps it would have been better to keep quiet? To just go long and not make a fuss? Yet we know inside that we took the proper course of action.

Even though outside it feels so painful. That is . . . until someone comes to us and thanks us for speaking up—saying they felt the same way. Admitting they didn't have the courage to come forward on their own.

We may begin to learn that our stand for what is right has affected far more people than we imagined. That the response we have seen so far is just the tip of the iceberg. So, even though many people may not appreciate what we did, there may be many who do.

Perhaps for a brief moment we can smile again and be encouraged to continue. And perhaps we can find a little bit of peace knowing we've helped someone we've never even met.

So, where can you stand up for something you feel is right and just? How can you be a beacon to those around you for a better way to live and treat others?

<u>PART FOUR</u>

OUR RELATIONSHIPS

CONNECTION, LOVE, AND
COMMUNITY

....

55

THE GREATEST DANCE WE DO IS THE DANCE BETWEEN HEAD AND HEART

There is a dance we all learn to do from a very young age.

It is not a physical dance, yet it is the most important dance we learn. It is the dance we do that takes us between our head and our heart.

Many experiences may teach us that being in our heart is not safe, so we flow up into our mind. And we stay there, sometimes for a very long time.

Until something special happens. We might meet someone or experience a great loss, and then suddenly we are back in our heart.

We've forgotten what it is like to feel. To truly connect with another seems awkward. Our heart is still tender from our previous heartbreak. Yet life puts us there.

And now we have a choice. We can choose to go back into our head and not feel—not feel the pain, the sadness, and the love—or we can open up to our heart. To all the emotions that have been stored up there. To reconnect with it so we can release that energy. And learn to open to something new. It may be something wonderful. It may be great joy and happiness. Or it can be something difficult and painful.

Regardless of what it is, at least we are feeling something. We may even feel it in our physical body. And that's the point . . . we need to feel again. To experience life again as it was meant to be experienced in full living emotion.

The mind is not bad. Neither is the heart. Learning the dance that we do between them, and why, is what is important. We have both and we need both. So, let's stop living as if it is one or the other. Let's learn the dance in which heart and head are the partners.

How comfortable are you going from your head to your heart?

....

56

HOME IS NOT OUR HOUSE, IT IS ABOUT LIVING IN THE HEART

Coming home is not about returning to our house or apartment. It is not about being with our family (although they can be there). It is not about visiting our place of birth or origin. It's about feeling the sense of home in our hearts. It's about feeling okay to be ourselves.

When we leave our center, our home, we lose ourselves. We become ungrounded. It becomes easy to get pulled into situations that do not need or deserve our attention.

When we get hurt, we close our hearts. It can take time to feel safe again and ready to reopen our hearts. To be back at the place where we are comfortable with ourselves.

Many things can take us away from our home. Our jobs, our businesses, our friends, our projects, our lovers. Finding our way back to our hearts can be an elusive endeavor. Especially when we have not traveled that way before.

While it is easy to leave the heart space, it is not as easy to reenter it.

When we feel unsafe and uncertain, moving back to center is frightening. We might get hurt again! We might be abused again! We might be left alone again! Yet the pain of not being home is actually worse than taking that risk.

Our souls desire to be back home. Every fiber of our being craves to be back home.

And when we reemerge in our true home, we *do* feel safe. Not because of what anyone else may do or not do. Because we are safe with ourselves.

Because this is where our true essence lies. Where our heart is, our home is.

Have you gone home lately? Have you connected with your heart lately?

57.

....

THERE IS NO THEM, THERE IS ONLY US

It is easy to fall into the trap of believing that there are "others" in this world, those who do not think the way we do, speak the way we do, or believe the things we do. We separate ourselves from other people where we see differences between them and us. But the truth is that we are more alike than we are different. We have more in common than divides us. For we are all people living on one planet. We are one human race, one species, and members of one global society.

When we learn to see people from this larger perspective, we will realize that we are all connected, if not in daily life, then by the very molecules that make up bodies, which come from stars that exploded long before we were born.

Where do you separate from others? Where do you divide, and can you instead find ways to bring people together?

58.

....

OUR PAIN IS HERE TO TEACH US WHERE WE CAN LOVE OURSELVES MORE

We all hurt sometimes. We feel the pain of loss or abandonment. And we shy away from the very pain that is a gift—for the pain we feel shows us where our inner work must occur. It points us in the direction of what we need to focus on next.

It calls us to look into ourselves and find a tender spot. The point from which the pain emanates. To find the true source of it.

So that we can heal. So that we can undo the patterns of thought and feeling that no longer serve us. So that we can bring a greater awareness to our lives.

If we dig underneath any pain we feel, we may find something else—something more basic, more primal—a wound that we never healed or acknowledged. A wound that we never shined a light on or knew was there.

By bringing a greater awareness to a wound, it no longer has to drive us. It may still be with us, yet it does not stop us.

We show that pain love, by loving ourselves.

We heal that pain by letting it know that it is okay to be a part of us.

And with our acceptance, we bring peace to it and peace to ourselves.

Pain is here to teach us so we can live more and love more, and so that, through our example, the world can too.

What pain are you holding on to? What is the source of the pain? Can you love the pain and see how it has served you?

....

59

HATE IS NOT ABOUT HATRED

Hate is not about hatred. Anger is not about rage. Fear is not about fright. When we go deeply enough, what underlies them all are pain and sadness.

When we are in pain, we lash out without thought or understanding. We may pick a specific target for our hate and anger, yet it is not about that specific target. It is about our pain. And underneath that pain is a profound sadness. In the moment, all we can feel is that if we cause someone or something else pain, it will take away ours.

Nothing is further from the truth. Pain only causes more pain. To stop the pain, we must be present to it, we must allow it to run its course without stuffing it down.

We all have pain and we all feel pain, the difference is how we deal with it. The most important thing is not to pass it on. So, let's give ourselves some space to feel our pain, to feel our sadness, and to allow our bodies to process it with time.

Perhaps when we learn not to pass on our pain, we will see less pain in the world.

Can you find a way not to pass on your own pain?

60.

....

WHEN WE ACCEPT UNCOMFORTABLE FEELINGS AS GIFTS, WE FIND LIBERATION

We all try to avoid them. Those uncomfortable feelings we feel sometimes. Those feelings of sadness, anger, grief, loneliness, and depression. Yet our desire to avoid them does not serve us for many reasons.

Mainly, it does not serve us because, whether or not we consciously feel them, they are there in our body—present in the nervous system. And their presence means they are affecting us regardless of whether we are aware of them or not.

The difference is that if we are present to them, we can release them much quicker, whereas if we deny their existence, they will linger, causing us to make decisions that might not be in our best interest, causing us to experience issues with our bodies or minds.

Being present to these feelings is the only way to process them, to keep them from turning into something physical, to stop them from causing an illness.

The illness may show up as a physical or emotional issue. What was once some sadness turns into full blown depression. What was once some anger turns into a disease that eats up the body.

To be present to the feelings is the first step toward wholeness. For when we are present to how we feel we can no longer ignore it. Then it is time to dig in deep.

Where do these feelings come from?

When did we first experience it?

How do they repeat in our lives?

What is the lesson and the beauty of it?

How has the feeling served us all these years?

While an uncomfortable feeling may seem like just a difficulty to overcome, all our uncomfortable feelings, in some way, have served us.

They protected us when we needed protection. They were the expression of something that was inside of us that needed to come out. If we stop judging these feelings and start accepting them as gifts, regardless of how comfortable or uncomfortable they may be to feel, we find liberation and peace.

So, what uncomfortable feelings come up for you? When have you felt them before? How have they served you in the past?

61.

....

TO TRULY CONNECT WITH OTHERS, WE MUST FIRST BE CONNECTED TO OURSELVES

How often do we take the time to truly connect with people? Do we allow ourselves to be present and open when with others?

Sometimes we can be in the same room with someone, yet not be present with them. If we really want to have connection, we need to do more than just spend time with someone, we need to be there, with them, and open to where they are in life. Without judgment or expectation. Without our own preconceptions of who they are. And it starts with us first.

Before we can be present with others, it is necessary to be present to ourselves. To our emotions. To our feelings. To our pain and our joy. To our anxiety and our fear. Why? Because only when we are present to our own feelings can we feel what others are feeling. Only then do we know how to relate to them on more than a superficial basis.

We know how we felt when we were in the midst of our own agony. We know what we wanted in that moment. So now we can give that to someone else.

We know what it is like to just want someone to be there to listen to us. Without being coached or cajoled. So now we can listen and be present to their pain. We can hold them as they cry and let their tears flow.

People will feel our presence so much more because they can feel how we are with them. And that shared presence makes all the difference. All the inner work we have done on ourselves will speak for itself, as our hearts open and we share the moment with our entire being.

Can you feel the connection when you are being truly present with someone?

62.

．．．．．．．．．．．．．．．．．．．．．．．．．．．．．．．

BETWEEN YOU AND I, THERE IS A LIVING, BREATHING FIELD

There is a relationship that exists between everything. Between us and the person across from us. Between ourselves and our partner.

And a third relationship that we often don't think about. That is the relationship to the third entity that is created between two or more people.

It gets created between a husband and wife. Between a parent and a child. Between a teacher and a student. Between any relationship of two or more individuals.

This third entity is very important. It is the glue that holds us together. Or breaks us apart. It is the force that creates communities, companies, and countries.

This entity of relationship lives in the field that is generated when we come together. Have you felt it? Have you acknowledged it? Have you looked at a relationship from the perspective of a third, living entity?

There is great value in adopting this perspective on relationships. When deciding if something is good for us, we can measure it with three different questions:

- Is it good for us?
- Is it good for the other person?
- Is it good for the relationship?

This is true whether it is a personal, business, or intimate relationship.

This new perspective, this new entity—if we treat it as a living, breathing being—we can then know what we need to do to support it. To grow it. To allow it to thrive.

We have all have relationships that have gone bad. Perhaps this perspective can help restore them?

What relationships do you have that can use some attention?

63

TRUE CONNECTION IS ABOUT PRESENCE

Connection is not just about mutual interests. Although that's a part of it.

Connection is not just about common beliefs. Although that's a part of it.

Connection is not just about shared experiences. Although that's a part of it.

Connection involves a deeper, more primal bonding. Does the other person feel safe to us? Can he protect me? Can she support me? Can we work together?

Can I trust them? Will they keep up their end of the bargain? Do they accept me for who I am? Can I accept them for who they are? Can we truly be present for each other?

Now that's a big one. Can we just be present with another person without judgment or expectation? When we can do that, we have true connection.

When we can just sit in someone's presence and be comfortable without having to do or say anything, that's real connection.

When we can just simply be with another human being, that's connection.

How do we get to that point? By just simply being with ourselves. If we can't be comfortable just being with ourselves, how can we be comfortable with someone else?

It all starts with us. Connecting with ourselves. Being present with ourselves without judgment or expectation. Then we can include someone else.

Then we can be truly present and connect with someone else.

Then we have the capacity to maintain, encourage, and grow the connection.

How connected are you with yourself? How connected are you with others?

64.

···

RELATIONSHIPS ARE ABOUT THE RELATIONSHIP WE HAVE WITH OURSELVES

Most of us spend a lot of time on our relationships. We work hard to make them work. Yet there is one relationship we often forget about and should not neglect. The relationship with ourselves.

We often feel that if someone breaks up with us there is something wrong with us.

Sometimes our parents don't agree with us and we wish we could make them see our side and believe in us.

Sometimes our friends do not treat us the way we want be treated and we think it is our fault.

In all three of these situations, we can easily forget what is most important. The primary relationship that affects all others.

The key to having a good relationship with anyone else is the relationship we secretly have with ourselves. How are we really feeling about ourselves? How do we talk to ourselves? How do we treat ourselves—especially when no one else is looking?

These are important things to look at. They determine how we show up in the world. They underlie all our interactions with other people.

Before we can have a strong relationship with another human being, we must first have a strong relationship with ourselves. We must show up for ourselves, take care of ourselves, value ourselves. For if we do not do any of these things, no one else will.

How could they? How could someone else treat us better than we treat ourselves?

And if someone did treat us better than we treat ourselves, would we be able to accept it?

If we do not feel worthy, confident, or at peace, how can being with someone else make us feel these things? It can't.

People can only distract us if we have an unsettled feeling inside. Most of us at times use our relationships to find what we are missing within ourselves. Yet this is a frustrating endeavor because no one else can fill us up.

Only we can fill up our own cup. Only we can give ourselves the acceptance we so look for. Only we can give ourselves the love, the kindness, the appreciation we so crave.

When we do, others can see it in us. They are drawn to it. And they reinforce it.

When we truly love ourselves, it becomes easy to find love. And when we don't, we just give it to ourselves.

No one wants to be lonely and alone all the time. Yet when we start by improving our relationship with ourselves, all other relationships improve. Without effort. Without intent.

When we are truly good with ourselves, then we naturally are good with others.

Can you see where your relationships are reflecting your relationship with yourself? Are there places you can have a better relationship with yourself?

65.

....

THE GROUP DYNAMIC IS ALWAYS A REFLECTION OF OUR INTERNAL DYNAMIC

When we work with others, as a profession or avocation, we sometimes think it's all about them. Actually, it's all about us.

When we work with a group, whether it's our tribe, our online following, or our bowling league, the group has come together because of common energy. The issues that arise are issues for everyone, in some way, not just an issue for one. It does not matter if you're a workshop facilitator, a healer, a shaman, an athletic coach, a teacher, or an executive consultant. The faces may look different, the clothes (or uniforms) may be far apart, yet the underlying energy and patterns are still present.

If we find ourselves getting annoyed at someone in the group who is not contributing or participating fully, then we must ask ourselves, *"How am I not contributing or participating?"*

If we notice someone not doing their work or ignoring homework for a class, we must ask, *"How am I not doing my own work?"*

The group reflects the individual and the individual reflects the group. It cannot be any other way, or else we would not be with that particular group or they would not be with us. The issues different members of a group are confronting may not be directly correlated. For example, perhaps the issue is that someone is being cheap with you. Even though you are generous with your friends, you have something in common— because you are cheap with yourself or your family. That's your version of the same issue. We just need to learn to be more figurative in our interpretations of our reflections, not quite so literal.

It is not easy to see our own issues reflected back to us in the behavior of other people. In fact, one of the hardest lessons to learn is that it's all our issue, in some manner.

Where do you see your issues reflected back to you? Where can you see what is going on inside of you showing up in the people around you?

66.

....

WHEN WE ADMIT BEING LOST, WE MAY FIND WE ARE NOT ALONE

I don't know what to do. These are six very difficult words for most of us to say. It doesn't feel safe to admit being uncertain. It is vulnerable and scary to be in that place. It seems as if we're expected to know what to do. That people depend on us knowing what to do.

We can feel like we have let everyone down when we don't know what to do. Yet when we admit it, it can bring us to a new place. A place of authenticity. A place of courage. A place of peace. Because when we admit not knowing, we find out something surprising.

We're not the only one.

There are lots of other people who don't know what to do, what to say, or where to go. And from that place of vulnerability, we find connection. We find comfort. We find that we're not alone.

When we open up and freely express that we're in an unfamiliar place in our lives, that we're lost and scared, the very thing we need in that moment shows up.

Other people. People who want to be there for us.

Not to do anything for us. Not to fix it and make it better. But just to be present with us. To hold our hand. To let us know that they feel the same way.

And with this connection comes relief. Because now we know that we're not alone. In fact, there are lots of people out there who feel the same way and they appreciate our openness.

Our rawness.

Our ability to express that we don't know what to do.

They can empathize and relate. We all feel that way sometime. We all find ourselves in unfamiliar situations without a compass or a map. Stuck in a place that we don't know how to get out of. And when we admit, the magic happens.

People show up and say, "Me too," and then, somehow, through some unknown force, we feel better, probably from just knowing that there is someone else there who feels as lost as we do. By them just being there, we no longer feel quite as lost.

Maybe, just maybe, we now can find our way out together.

So where in your life would it serve you to say, "*I just don't know*"?

67.

....

OUR RELATIONSHIP TO THE RELATIONSHIP IS MORE IMPORTANT THAN WE REALIZE

Relationships are tricky things. We often find ourselves in relationships that aren't working. Sometimes we have no idea why.

Is it all about the other person?

Is it all about ourselves?

Is it about both of us?

Or is it about something else?

Perhaps there is a different perspective we can take. A different way of looking at relationships that can helps us to be better. What about our relationship to the relationship?

We often forget that when two people come together, something more is created: The relationship.

What is our relationship to the actual relationship? Are we being in service to the other person or to the relationship? Are we paying attention just to the other person or do we pay attention to the relationship itself?

How do we feel about the relationship? Are we joyful? Are we sad? Are we tired? Are we irritated?

Not to the other person. To the relationship itself.

Could we be more playful with the relationship? Could we cherish and adore the relationship?

It's not just about the other person. It's not just about ourselves. It's about everyone involved and their individual relationship to the relationship. Whether it is a business relationship, a family relationship, or an intimate relationship.

When we consider how we relate to the relationship we are in, we see things differently, from a different perspective. When we look at it differently, we can create something different. A more vibrant relationship. A healthier relationship. A more joyful relationship.

Not a relationship to or with the other person but with the relationship itself.

So, how are you feeling about your relationships?

68.

....

BY APPRECIATING MORE AND COMPARING LESS, WE ENRICH OUR LIVES

We spend a great deal of time comparing ourselves to others. We think:

He's so much taller than I am.

She looks so much thinner than I am.

They have a bigger house than we do.

But these comparisons rarely bring us peace or joy. We often feel as if we're coming up short when we think:

Do you think she's prettier than me?

He looks like he makes more money than I do.

Look at that new car, it must run so much better than ours.

How we feel depends on which side of the comparative equation we are on. Sometimes we come out on top. Yet even when we temporarily make ourselves feel better by comparing ourselves favorably with another person, in the long run, there's always someone who has something nicer, bigger, or better than we do.

Do you think this restaurant is better than the other one?

Do you like this movie better than the one last year?

Is this book a better read than that one?

Especially when we compare two things that are not directly comparable, we set ourselves up for disagreement.

How about thinking instead, *They are both good in different ways?*

How about, *I enjoyed both equally for different reasons?*

How about, *For where I was at that time in my life it was perfect, and now that I'm at a different place, this is perfect instead?*

Many factors go into what is good/ better/best at a specific time. By comparing different things that all have something to contribute we diminish each one. But when we learn to see everything as having value in its own way, we add to each one. When we stop comparing and start seeing things in their own light, we can appreciate diverse things.

Yes, there are times when comparison can be useful.

Yet perhaps we can enrich our lives by appreciating more and comparing less.

Do you notice when you are comparing yourself to someone else? How does it make you feel? Can you appreciate the differences instead of making a value judgment about them?

69.

....

PRESENCE LEADS US TO CONNECTION, WHICH BRINGS US TO COMMUNITY

Why is it we have more ability to connect to people, yet feel less connected? We can talk or text with anyone in the world. We can meet people online with the exact same interests. And we are still more isolated and feel less a part of a community than ever before.

Could it be that we are less connected with ourselves? Perhaps we are so distracted that we can't feel our own emotions? Is that why we often feel more comfortable texting someone far away than being in the same room with them?

Is it fear? Is it a lack of presence? Or is it something else? Something subtler at work? Maybe it is more about not wanting to be vulnerable, or about what feels safe and easy to do.

It can be scary to expose ourselves to the people right in front of us. It takes some courage to open up and talk to the person in the room who could challenge you. We like to avoid confrontation because confrontation feels uncomfortable, so we lean towards comfort than challenge.

We often take the path of least resistance when it comes to connection, so we text someone we don't really know that well rather than talk to someone who sees us every day, yet that really doesn't serve us, for community is far more important than most of us realize.

Community nurtures us. Community supports us. Community holds us in a way that raises us up energetically— so we can contribute more. So that we can create more. So that we can cry and laugh and feel more. So that we can be safe and be heard and be who we are.

The person in front of us sees us far more than anyone on the other side of a phone or a computer. They can feel us as we can feel them, and that is valuable.

Let us lean, therefore, into community. Lean into presence. Lean into connection. And see what unfolds for us as we feel that we are more a part of the human race.

So, what can you do to be more present with people?

70.

························

TRUST IS MORE PRECIOUS THAN THE MOST VALUABLE GEM

It is not easy to trust someone. Trust is something we build up over time. Trust comes with the presence we feel from the other.

And trust is a sacred bond. When someone trusts us, we must take it very seriously. Whether they are trusting us with their time, their money, or their secrets. They are putting us in a very honored position. One that is delicate and sensitive. For that trust can be easily broken by the slip of a word, or a careless gesture.

People trust us because we are trustworthy. Yet to remain trustworthy can be difficult. There are temptations to break that trust. To share what they told us in confidence to someone else. To take just a little something that isn't ours because they will never notice it. To tell that little (or big) white lie because they will never find out.

And then they do. And trust is broken. Sometimes beyond repair.

We break the trust placed in us because we don't value it enough. Because we don't understand the sacredness with which it was given to us.

When we deeply understand that there is no currency greater than trust, we will treat it very differently, respecting it immensely and holding it as more precious than the most valuable gem. Indeed, trust is like the finest crystal glass in the world. Beautiful to behold, yet once it is broken it can never be restored exactly the way it was before.

When someone trusts us enough to follow us, to work with us, to give us access to their heart and their dreams, it is the greatest gift of all.

Where do people trust you? How precious you take that trust? Can you cherish it a little bit more?

71.

....

WE CAN TRULY HELP OTHERS WHEN WE COME FROM A PLACE OF JOY

Many of us are called to be in service to others. To help others heal. To support them in their growth. But there is something to be careful of when we are.

For it is quite easy to use helping other to distract us from doing our own work to heal ourselves, to look at our own internal processes and to take time to care to nurture ourselves.

It is quite appealing to focus on others. After all, look how much worse off they are compared to us. We know what they need. We see things so clearly for them. We want to help. And we do.

Yet it is easy to forget about ourselves in the process. We put our own needs to the side. We put everyone else first and ourselves last. And that is a recipe for a crash. For we cannot continue to only help others without taking care of our own needs. Our own growth. Our own healing.

In the end, all healing is self-healing. All growth is self-growth.

To be in service is a beautiful thing, as long as we don't forget to fill up our own cup first and ensure that we are giving from a place of overflow rather than from a place of scarcity. A place of true inner peace and not a place of avoidance.

It is seductively easy to keep our attention on others and lose our own opportunity to heal and grow. Yet when we focus on our own path first, helping others becomes easier. We have a new perspective and can see things more clearly.

We can help, as long as we are truly helping from a place of joy, not distraction.

Can you joyfully help others? Have you filled up your own cup first?

72.

....

TO BE KIND TO OTHERS IS TO GIVE OURSELVES A GREAT GIFT

There are many ways to show up. We can show up with kindness. We can show up with coldness. How we show is more about us than the situation.

The circumstances may be difficult to deal with. They may not be what we want them to be. So, we should remember that if we come from a place of blaming or victimization, we feel worse, whereas if we come from a place of love and peace, we not only feel better, the people around us do too.

We often get triggered when people are not kind or gentle with us. We take it personally. We feel betrayed. And that makes it hard to come from a gentle and loving place.

The reason to show up in a different way is not about the other person or the situation. It is about what it does to us. It is about the difference we make to ourselves. It is about being kind and gentle with ourselves.

Being angry, hateful, and vengeful may make us feel more powerful in the moment. However, when things settle down, when we have some perspective, when we take some time to feel into what is really going on inside of us, we discover it is not who we are.

Showing up angry is not how our soul and our heart truly wants to express itself. It only hurts us.

On the other hand, to come from a place of peace and joy is not only for the benefit of others. It is first and foremost for our own benefit. For how it makes us feel. For what it does to our bodies. For the effect it has on our own chemistry and nervous system.

To be free from the anxiety that we feel when we get triggered by others, we can come from a higher place. From a different perspective. From a broader view of the situation.

We can rise above the immediate and see things from elevated view. It looks much different from up there. This difference can make our lives beautiful and change the world.

How can you change your world with kindness?

PART FIVE

OUR TRUTH

STORY, WORDS, AND VIBRATION

73.

························

OUR ENTIRE LIFE IS DETERMINED BY THE STORIES WE TELL OURSELVES

There is one thing that so powerful it can change our life. There is a secret weapon that when utilized properly can make a failure a success. It is something that with just one little adjustment, one little change, everything in our world changes.

That one dynamic, potent, universal thing is the story we tell ourselves about our life, about our relationships, and about our experiences. The story we tell ourselves about our past, our present, and our future. The story we replay inside our heads about who we are, what we are, and how we are. The story that justifies, defends, and protects.

The real secret is . . . it's just a story! And because it's just a story and we are its author means that we are capable of telling a new story.

Don't like the circumstances you are in? Tell a new story!

Don't like the relationships you are in? Tell a new story!

Don't like the family you are in? Tell a new story!

It does not matter if your new story is true or not, you can make it true. It does not matter if your new story is realistic or not, you will make it a reality. It does not matter if your new story has happened yet or not, just keep telling it and it will happen.

Are we telling ourselves stories of how we are worthy or unworthy? Good or not good enough? Lovable or unlovable?

Let's shift the stories rolling around inside our heads to be more supportive to us and see what shifts and changes in our life.

What is a story you would like to tell yourself about who you are?

From the moment we are born we begin to create stories around our experiences. We start to label events as *good* or *bad*. We then reflect on those judgments and make them mean something.

I'm a bad person because I don't like what happened to me.

Life is good because I got something I wanted.

People love me because they give me attention.

The world sucks because someone hurt me.

All of these thoughts are stories that may not have anything to do with the factual events but these stories hold great power over us as we make significant meaning from them about our lives.

I'm worthless.

I can't do anything right.

I'm a failure.

These stories soon become our identity, and we unconsciously find ways to live into these identities.

My life is blessed.

I always find a way.

I can do anything I set my mind to.

It doesn't matter if these stories support us or disempower us, they are programs we run over and over in our heads as we encounter new situations. The truth of our programs is apparent in our experience.

Stories are only true because we believe them and have made meaning from them. The way to use this to our advantage is to remember that *it is all made up*! We created the meaning and we can change it if we wish, anytime. A black cat walking in front of us doesn't have to mean something bad will happen to us. We can decide it means that animals love us.

Armed with this recognition, our life is no longer dependent on the stories we created a long time ago. We are empowered to pick meanings for things in our life that uplift us and keep us strong.

What in your life would you like to make a new meaning for?

74.

....

COMMUNICATION IS THE KEY TO ALL OF OUR RELATIONSHIPS

You've heard it before, but it bears repeating: Communication is key!

It is the key to all of our relationships for a number of reasons regardless of the situation, the relation-ship, or the business.

Most of the time we think we know what another person has meant and we think they know exactly what we meant when we had a conversation. Yet, if we check in with each other weeks, days, or even hours later, we may find that our understanding is not as clear or as accurate as we thought it was.

More relationships have been broken, more partnerships have dissolved, more businesses have been lost because communication was insufficient or not maintained as time went on, and things heard were not repeated for clarity, than from any other cause.

It is helpful when having a breakdown of commun-ication to remember that miscommunication does not happen on purpose. We do not intend to misunderstand someone; nor they us. What we hear is merely a reflection of where our consciousness is at a given time. We sometimes forget that things change over time and with those changes come our perceptions of what that means to our original communication.

The solution is always the same. Communicate often, communicate constantly, and revisit all communication over time. It may save us more than a few headaches.

So, where can you be communicating more in your life? At home? At the office? With a friend?

75.

....

BECAUSE WE ARE IMPERFECT, OUR COMMUNICATION IS IMPERFECT

Communication is inherently imperfect. The words we use and even how we say them are always open to interpretation. As human beings, we make mistakes all the time about what was meant or even what was said. Therefore, to expect things to go perfectly all the time is unrealistic.

If we commit to staying present to a conversation, we can come to a mutual understanding. We can clarify and correct. We can see where the perception is different from our intention. And we can add further communication to improve the understanding.

The one thing we cannot afford to do is decrease the amount of communication we are having. This may be uncomfortable at times. It may take extra effort to stay present at times. But we really must do it if we value clarity and mutual understanding. When we decide to withdraw and decrease or stop our communication, that's when real trouble begins.

Should we choose to stop communicating, we can be blocked to understanding what is really going on. When we close up and stop interacting with another person, then nothing between us can move forward.

It does not matter who we think is right or wrong. It does not matter who was justified or not. The conversation and the possibilities all end the moment we decide that it is no longer worth communicating. That's how most relationships end. Without communication, there can be no relationship.

If we can do the difficult work of staying open, of being present to the conversation regardless of how we feel about the other person. Then, something can move. Then, there is at least some hope. Then, we can change the outcome and work through whatever it was that was bothering us. We can't do any of that if we clam up and go away.

The amazing thing is that when we stay present and continue to communicate, most disagreements can be worked out. Most of the time we will find out that we misunderstood what was said or meant. Or they will.

The important thing is not who was right or wrong. The important thing is that we stuck around to talk it through until either there was some resolution or there was a mutual agreement about an ending. Either way, everyone involved felt better knowing that they had done everything they could to work it out.

Sometimes we have to walk away. But many times, we just have to stay present and keep talking.

Can you see where you stop communicating too soon? Is there a conversation that you need to reopen?

76

THE SOLUTION TO MISUNDERSTANDING IS GREATER COMMUNICATION

How good are we at communicating? Do we listen more than we talk? Are we present in our conversations? Do we make assumptions that get us in trouble?

Inevitably, bad communication leads to misunderstandings. Learning to avoid assumptions, or at least to verify our assumptions is a great place to start. Communicating more, not less, is the key.

We think we talk enough with people, but do we really? Speaking with people is not all about us expressing ourselves. It's about listening to the other person and truly hearing what they are saying without judgment or being defensive. When we project our own interpretation on a conversation we may get in trouble. But if we take the time to verify what the other person is trying to convey, we gain understanding.

The times when we make up conversations in our head what is said often has nothing to do with reality. The only sure-fire solution to avoiding misunderstandings is to communicate often. Communicate frequently. Communicate more than you think is necessary.

The better the communication between people, the better the connection, the better the understanding.

Is there some misunderstanding in your life that can be cleared up with more communication?

....

77

THE QUALITY OF OUR LIVES IS DETERMINED BY THE QUALITY OF THE QUESTIONS WE ASK

How often do we listen to the questions we ask ourselves in our heads? How often are these questions that cannot be answered? How does it affect how we feel about ourselves?

When we start to become more conscious and mindful, we start to observe ourselves more. We notice little things, such as how we may ask questions like: *"Why does this always happen to me?"* This is not a particularly helpful question to ask, for it feeds the unconscious mind, which then goes to work trying to find an answer.

This is a very powerful form of negative programming because when we ask questions that will inevitably lead to negative answers, it disempowers us.

The solution is to ask more empowering questions—ones that actually serve us—like: *"How can this serve me?"* or *"How can I have fun with this?"* Such questions point our minds in a direction that creates a better life for ourselves.

In general, *why* questions do not serve us. *How* and *what* questions are much more constructive. So, as we notice ourselves asking questions that do not serve us, we can learn to reframe them into questions that move us forward.

"How does this help me?"

"What can I do to improve this situation?"

"Where can I find more resources to help me with this challenge?"

These three good questions can move us closer to an answer that will actually help us to find real solutions to the things we face in life. As we become more adept at asking high-quality questions, the quality of our life improves.

What high-quality questions can you start asking yourself today?

....

78

MORE IS SAID WITH OUR PRESENCE THAN OUR WORDS

Communication is about more than words. It is about more than our voice, more than the music we make or the body language we use. Communication is a practice.

It is a practice of using our whole being.

It is a practice of presence.

It is a practice of attention.

It is a practice of feeling.

It is a practice of focus.

When we communicate, we are engaged with another in a precious way. They are giving their time and attention to us. They are giving of themselves to us.

It is up to us to honor that gift. And we honor it by being fully present with them. To see them, feel them, and experience them deeply.

This way they see us, feel us, and experience us deeply too.

It is a holy communion. A sacred moment.

We honor that sacred moment through the quality of our contact with the other person. We honor it by standing fully in our own presence and by fully taking in their presence. When we truly show up this way for another person, they can feel it.

More gets conveyed through how we are being with them—more feeling, more energy, more information—than we convey merely by speaking. We say so much with our presence.

What is your presence saying about you?

79.

....

NOT GIVING THE ANSWER ALLOWS PEOPLE TO GROW AND TRUST THEMSELVES

How do we empower others? How do we, as coaches, teachers, guides, parents, bosses, and managers, help those we interact with, find their way?

Do we give them all the answers? Do we tell them all that we have learned? Or do we guide them to find the answers within themselves?

Handing someone the solution to a problem they are facing may feel good to us, yet if the people we are trying to help do not learn to find answers on their own, we have disempowered, rather than empowered them.

Being a real guide, a true mentor, means learning to ask the questions that allow them to realize what the correct path is for themselves.

We may think we know the answer. We may think we have the solution they need. Yet if all we do is share our opinions with them, they aren't discovering how to access their own inner wisdom. We are not teaching them that they have the power to resolve their issues on their own. We are not giving them the gift of our presence and allowing them to use their creativity and trust themselves more.

It does not matter whether the person we are working with is our partner, our lover, our child, our employee, or our co-worker. It does not matter how important or unimportant the situation may be. We are only either encouraging the people around us to forge their own path through their efforts or we are taking that opportunity away from them.

When we create dependency upon us in others, we create followers. When we create the atmosphere for independent thinking, we allow people to grow into leaders.

Which do you want to create? Followers or fellow leaders?

80.

....

INVESTING IN KINDNESS
YIELDS MANY RETURNS OF JOY

We all think about the return we get on what we spend. If we invest our time into a project, what's the payoff? If we invest our money, what's the rate of return?

Yet how do we measure the return on our kindness? Do we know truly how our kindness affects other people? Can we see all the ripples that it generates? Do we give our kindness away to receive something? Or is it just because it is the proper thing to do?

What is truly amazing is to see how those who give their kindness away without any thought of getting a return on it, often get so much back in return. Perhaps a small act of kindness is captured on camera by someone watching and the video goes viral. Perhaps we once did an act of kindness for a friend in need and when we are in need that friend shows up and is there for us when we least expect it. Or perhaps our acts of kindness create a kind community around us.

It is hard to know how the seeds we plant will sprout. These seeds of kindness we plant not for our personal gain but just for the sake of helping others—to shine some light in a dark place. For the sake of our sense of doing the right thing.

Kindness sometimes feels so good in the moment. Because we wish someone had been kind to us when we were in a similar situation in the past, we may relish in creating a moment of joy in someone's life.

This creates a moment of joy for us too. That's the real return on investment when it comes to kindness. We invest in kindness to create more joy. And then it ripples outward through them creating more joy for others, even for people we don't know.

So, is it worth investing in kindness even if we don't see a return? Absolutely!

What acts of kindness could you create today?

81.

··

JUST BECAUSE WE FEEL ANGRY DOES NOT MEAN WE HAVE TO RESPOND WITH ANGER

There is a misconception about people who are kind. About people who normally don't get upset at others. About people who treat others with kindness and compassion.

Even kind people get angry.

Even kind people get upset sometimes.

Even kind people feel like pounding the wall on occasion.

The difference between kind people and those who are not as kind is that anger is not their default state of being. Not their preferred way of interacting. They see the disadvantages of acting out of anger or rage, and they choose to avoid them.

This does not mean they don't feel the anger or get riled up. This does not mean they don't feel like fighting, just that they look for a different way of expressing themselves—a more productive way. A way that can avoid the escalation of emotions.

When anger is met with anger, it rarely leads to a productive outcome. It rarely serves either person involved. And it often creates situations that can easily spiral out of control. Which leads us to make decisions and say things we regret later. It causes us to act in ways that once we calm down, we don't even understand ourselves.

Of course, we all get angry sometimes.

Of course, we all experience anger in our own way.

Yet it is a conscious choice how we decide to respond to it or interact with people when we're angry. How we move forward with it is a decision.

Not responding out of anger is the surest way to deescalate matters. It is like putting water on a fire. Things stop burning out of control and we can begin to talk more calmly and rationally.

Another person may still be angry. And we may be too. But this does not mean we have to be unkind or vicious. We can be compassionate both to ourselves and to the other person no matter how we feel inside.

We still have to deal with those feelings and release that energy. We just don't have to release it in front of the other person.

Managing our angry feelings responsibly is what kind people do.

Is there some anger you need to express? How can you release it without reacting in front of the other person?

82.

....

TO HEAL OUR DEEPEST WOUNDS, WE MUST SPEAK THE TRUTH ABOUT OUR PAIN

In order to begin a healing process, there is something we must be willing to do. It is not just about taking better care of ourselves or changing our lifestyle. It is about something far deeper and more difficult. To start a journey to wholeness we must be willing to speak our truth.

This is the truth about how we feel deep inside. The truth about our pain and suffering. The truth about our desires and secret wishes. Without admitting to ourselves what we are experiencing, feeling, and truly want to have happen now, we cannot move forward.

What we hide inside us will continue to control us. What we shun and fear will continue to affect our life. The truth we deny will fester and grow until it comes out.

It is not easy to admit the truth to ourselves. It takes courage to be brutally honest about how we feel and what we want. Yet we do it not for others, but for ourselves, so that we may be whole again and at peace.

It is only by shining the light of our own truth into the blackest corners of our soul that we free ourselves from the shackles of the deepest wounds that stay with us our whole lives. These are the wounds that kill us if we do not address them. These are the wounds that drive us if we do not speak them out loud.

What is your truth that you have been afraid to speak? What pain is in there that needs to come out?

83.

························

THERE IS A NEW PATH ON THE OTHER SIDE OF THAT AWKWARD CONVERSATION

We all avoid having uncomfortable conversations, the ones where we know will feel awkward and where we are not sure of the outcome. Avoidance keeps us from experiencing something amazing. It keeps us from finding out what is on the other side. It stops us from the gold that is underneath the surface waiting to be dug up.

Perhaps you already had one conversation, and there was something left unsaid. You knew at the time that there was more to it, yet you didn't ask. And because you didn't explore, the real conversation didn't happen.

The good news is that there is usually another opportunity. You can still reach out.

The key to finding a new path is for us to go where we didn't go last time. To be nervous and still say what wasn't said last time. To ask for what we want and didn't speak up about before. The truly amazing thing about doing this is that most of the time the answers we receive are not what we have expected. In fact, an answer can be the complete opposite of what we expect, or something that takes us in such a different direction that it never came to mind. And that now we're having a whole new conversation, one that takes us to an undiscovered country where now we are free to create something new and different.

Or perhaps we learn that it really is time to move on. That the path we were on before has truly come to an end. So now we know and we are free to start a new path.

Regardless of the direction of a difficult conversation, it will bring something new into our lives. It will liberate us from the fear that kept us from asking in the first place. And we will grow and transform as we move forward in our lives. We may even look back on that the trepidation that kept us from asking to talk in the first place and wonder why we waited such a long time?

Is there a difficult conversation you've been off? Can you now approach it with an air of excitement of what might be on the other side of that conversation?

84.

························

OUR WOUNDS ARE OUR EXCUSE TO HIDE IN PLAIN SIGHT

We have a tendency to hold on to our pain. Often, we have had the pain for so long that we don't remember what it is like not to have it and it feels scary to let it go.

There is a benefit to holding onto pain that isn't discussed too often. That benefit is how pain gives us the perfect excuse ... The perfect excuse not to do something. The perfect excuse not to show up. The perfect excuse not to try.

We can use our pain in so many ways. We can use it as the reason why not to be vulnerable. Or we can use it as the reason to be vulnerable. To transform and change.

We use our pain all the time. Usually, we are not even aware of it. It is something that just sits there in the back of our consciousness and we think we are showing up for others, yet we are just hiding in plain sight.

We are present.

Yet we are not really present.

We are showing up.

Yet we are not really showing up.

We show up in our wound.

We may even talk about our wound.

In fact, we may wallow in our wound.

Yet we are not moving past our wound because to move past our wound is scary. It has been our companion for so many years and comforted us when we fail.

Sometimes old pain keeps us safe so we don't have to be hurt again.

The trouble is that when we just live in our wound, we are not being true to ourselves. We are not being who we really are. We are not living authentically—and freshly or in the moment. We are not showing up as our best selves. We use the identity related to old pain to hide from being who we can truly be.

And who we truly are is a gift to the world.

It is our presence that lights the way for others to see that they can get past their wounds as well, drop their excuses, and stop hiding in plain sight too.

Can you see where in your life you are hiding in plain sight because of your pain?

85.

....

TO BE HONEST WITH OTHERS, WE MUST FIRST BE HONEST WITH OURSELVES

Being truthful is not about telling the truth to others. Being truthful is not not-telling lies. Being truthful is about being honest with yourself.

Now, before we can begin to be authentic in public, we must get into alignment within ourselves. How, for instance, can we speak truth to a tribe of followers if we do not even know it ourselves?

Too many people say one thing in private and another in public. Regardless of the validity of the statements, if we are not sharing the same message in private and in public, we are not being truthful.

Does this mean we have to tell everyone everything? No, of course not. What it means is that we are clear in our intent and with our presence. It means we are being the same person with our families, our friends, our business associates, and our tribe. Our essence is what matters.

Our presence conveys our essence. Our words reflect our essence.

The truer to ourselves about ourselves we are, the truer we can be with other people.

Is there someplace in your life you can be truthful to yourself? Can you see where you've been not completely honest with yourself?

86.

····································

OUR OWN FEAR CAUSES US TO HIDE OUR BRILLIANT LIGHT

There is this place inside of us where we hide.

We hide our own special form of crazy. We hide our uniqueness and our innocence. We hide the best parts of us because we have been taught to. Through experience, we've learned that it is not safe to be ourselves or show our true colors.

We sometimes believe it's not safe to admit to our friends or our partners how we really feel. Our experiences also have shown us that others won't accept us for being different.

The kids at school may have been merciless. The neighborhood bullies may have tried to make sure we would never feel safe again. Yet there comes a time in all our lives when our soul drives us to break free. Break free from trauma. Break free from oppression. Break free and let our wings unfurl so we may fly.

It takes bravery to stop hiding. To let ourselves be seen. It takes us allowing ourselves to feel scared again. It takes facing the fact that we just might be rejected again. When we're ready, we do it anyway. We stand up and give ourselves permission to be who we really are.

We cast off our concerns about what others may think.

We rid ourselves of the habit of pleasing others over ourselves.

We speak our truth.

We express our individual nature.

We allow our light to shine as it was meant to.

Where can you allow your light to shine again? Or perhaps just shine a little brighter?

89.

························

WE FIND OUR VOICE WHEN WE SHARE OUR WORDS, OUR ACTIONS, AND OUR PRESENCE

We often hear people talk about finding their voice, but what exactly does it mean? Our voice is not about how we pronounce our words or the content we share. Finding our voice means showing up and then, through our actions and in what we say, convey that we are here and have something to share.

Finding your voice is not about talking a lot or about telling someone what to do. It's about courage, about standing out from the crowd and allowing our light to shine on others for a few moments. It's definitely not about ego or about how great we are. It comes down to being humble and brave, and sharing what we've learned for ourselves.

Using our voice means showing up when we commit to showing up and sharing our spirit and energy with those who choose to listen to us. What we say may or may not touch people. It may or may not inspire people. What we say may mean something very deep to another person or it may mean nothing at all to anyone except ourselves. It means we speak our truth regardless of who we're talking to or what they think of it.

We can speak our truth in many different ways. We speak our truth with our actions and our presence as much as we speak it with our voice.

Is there somewhere in your life you feel the need to share? Is there someplace in your life you can express yourself where have not expressed yourself before?

90.

···

WE CAN BE RIGHT OR HAPPY, BUT RARELY BOTH

We never really win an argument. No matter how hard we try to convince the other person that they are wrong, they will only dig in their heels. If anything, they will only be more convinced they are right. And if by some miracle we do get them to concede that we are right and they are wrong, they will remain angry at us. If we lose, we lose. If we win, we lose.

Perhaps because we are playing the wrong game?

Maybe what we should be concerned with is not winning but being happy.

The old adage is "You can be right or you can be happy but rarely both."

If we change our focus from winning to being happy, we can play a totally different game and play in a totally different way. Because now it is not about the end result but about how we play. When we give up our need to be right and focus on our desire to be happy, we can joyfully skip down the road. We can let others have whatever opinions they want to have.

As long as we're happy, who cares?

Being in a joyful place will cause others to wonder why we are so happy. Maybe then we can start a movement and they also will give up the need to be right and focus on being happy instead. That is how we all can win.

So, let's stop playing the win-lose type of game and learn to play more win-win games.

After all, aren't they much more fun?

PART SIX

OUR VISION

AWARENESS, DISCERNMENT, AND
INTENTION

91.

....

ALL OF LIFE IS LIVED IN THE PRESENT MOMENT

Living in the future is easy. We all do it sometimes. We look forward to an event or goal and allow it to consume our attention until that special day arrives. Then the future is here. We have made our goal or accomplishment.

Now what do we do? We set another goal! Which is all fine and dandy unless it keeps us from living in the present.

When we live in the present we can still march towards our goals. Yet we are more aware of our steps. We see more of our surroundings. We feel more of the wind on our face.

When we are truly being present to our lives, we are fully engaged. We pay attention to the here and now.

When we live in the future, we put off our enjoyment. We delay happiness. We forgo our peace and live as if we are constantly running—not an external running, but an internal running.

We are always longing for the next big thing. The next shiny object. The next promotion.

When we are present, we are living our lives to the fullest. We are happy, sad, joyful, terrified, anxious, and much more and we feel all of it. We feel it deeply in our whole body.

This can be scary and exhilarating. Mostly though, it is just what is feels like to be alive.

We can share our presence with those we love in a manner that truly serves. And we can revel in the moments that make us feel amazing.

It is all here waiting for us in the present moment.

How can you be more aware of the present moment? Can you see what you do to take yourself out of presence?

92.

....

BEING STUCK IS A GREAT OPPORTUNITY TO PONDER LIFE MORE DEEPLY

Feeling stuck is an uncomfortable feeling. We all want to move forward, take action, and get on to the next big thing. Yet sometimes being stuck is exactly where we need to be.

There is great information in being in that place of *stuckness*. Perhaps it is an indication that we can take a break. Perhaps it is a way for the Universe to slow us down and give us some perspective. Maybe we need to be stuck every once in a while, to remind us of what it's like and why we like moving forward so much more.

There is so much to be learned from being in a stuck place, if we are okay with not being comfortable in that place, give it some space, and look at it with new eyes.

Is there another way to go?

Are we sure we want to continue on the path we're on? Is there a new direction or new journey we could take that would feel better for us? Are there things we have not yet considered about where we are that we could look at more deeply?

Being stuck is one of the great pauses we can take to look around, reevaluate, and reconsider what we're doing or where we're going. So, let's not waste the moment complaining about it. Let's use being stuck as the great opportunity it is to ponder and meditate on our situation more deeply.

So, where are you stuck in life? What opportunity lies there for you to see things deeper?

93.

....

EVERY NEW DAWN IS A CHANCE TO SEE THE WORLD WITH NEW EYES

What if everything we think we know is wrong? What if our history is incorrect? What if the basic assumptions we base our life on are just not right? Could we face up to the truth and go on living? Could we admit that we've been wrong about our beliefs and face life anew? Could we see the world with new eyes, letting go of all we believe is true?

It takes both a strong will and an open heart to hear something that challenges everything we've held dear. In today's changing world, where information is being revealed to us at a breakneck pace, this is exactly what we have to contend with. Our view of the history of the planet is constantly being challenged as new discoveries show that life is much older than we first thought. New scientific evidence is showing that the start and evolution of the Universe might not be what has been accepted for so long.

In our individual lives, our views of our ancestors and parents change over time. Now that people are living longer, we see things differently. Our perspective as a race is changing. Everything around us seems to be morphing. The interconnectedness of life is more evident to us than ever before.

Technological development is turning science fiction into fact. The cell phone of today was once a fantasy device on a TV show. Technology as we know it is improving at a pace where what changes in a single lifetime formerly took generations to achieve. So, how can we feel confident that we really know what is going on? How can we hold on to old beliefs so tightly in the face of radical change? How can we stay the same when everything around us is mutating at light speed?

The time has come to release our grip on assumptions that have ruled our lives for generations on how things were and how they will be. The time has come to look at each new day as if it means we are living in a brand-new world, a brand-new reality. Because that is where we live.

Every day we are faced with a new reality based on new discoveries and experiences. Perhaps looking at our personal history and letting go of the stories we and our family have long lived by would be good for us.

It would be good for us to let go of the meanings we have made of experiences that no longer serve us. To wake up each day and release something old in our minds and hearts. To be as a child who knows it knows nothing. And to be open to life bringing us whatever it brings us without judgment or reservation.

What a beautiful journey awaits us in this new world.

So where can you let go of some long-held beliefs and see life with brand new eyes?

94.

....

INTENTION AND INFLECTION ARE THE FOUNDATION OF ALL THAT WE DO

The intention with which we do anything is very powerful. It creates the energy that is the foundation of all our actions. It is like the inflection we use when we speak. The same word can have two totally different meanings depending on our tone of voice.

Are we doing something out of a feeling of guilt or shame? Or out of joy and contribution? Are we looking to serve and help others, or are we out for our benefit? Are we giving from a place of abundance and flow, or is it a transaction that we are waiting for the return on? Of course, more often than not, our intentions are mixed and not purely one thing or another. That's okay, as long as we are aware of it.

Knowing what our main intention and our secondary intentions are is valuable. Often, we can see how they play out in our interactions with others and most obviously in our results. Awareness is the first step to understanding and making a change to how we do anything. Instead of running by default, we can be more intentional with our actions by taking the time to be quiet and think and feel about what we are about to engage in.

Does this action we are about to take make us feel good deep inside? Does it make us feel that we are a creator and not a victim? Does is reflect our power and our beauty or our fear and our pain?

Determining our intention is a powerful first step, we just have to take the time to make it a priority in our life.

So, what is your intention?

95.

....

OUR FUTURE LIES IN THE VISION WE HOLD FOR OURSELVES

What is it that pulls us forward into a better life? It is not a better job or a better partner. It is not more money or more contacts. It is the vision we hold of our future selves.

How we envision ourselves in our future is what pulls us forward. It calls us to do more, be more, and serve more. When we can imagine ourselves not only achieving more in our lives, but contributing more to the lives around us, it inspires us to become more of who we really are. We can only grow to the extent that we envision ourselves changing. We only strive to the level that our mind's eye can see as achievable for us.

Our life is a creation of the vision we hold for ourselves and our belief that this vision is real and possible.

Can you see yourself a week, a month, or a year into the future? Can you see the beauty you will create, the good you will do, the inspiration you will spread?

It is time to envision it more, feel it more, and allow it to pull you forward.

96.

VISION AND FAITH GO HAND IN HAND AND ARE ESSENTIAL FOR US TO CREATE

Some say faith is believing in what we cannot see.

Often, faith is relegated to the realm of the religious or spiritual. Yet, do we not all have to have faith in our vision and our goals in order to move forward? Do we not have to have faith in ourselves and our abilities in order to create something new?

Believing only in what we can see externally does not mean we cannot see things that are not yet there internally. Indeed, creation always starts with an internal vision for what we desire to bring into this world.

Is our vision of a new business, a new building, or a new organization to feed the poor?

Do we not have a vision for what our lives will look like in a few days, a few weeks, or a few years?

If we do not have faith enough in our vision, we put no effort into it. Vision and faith must go hand in hand for us to move forward with creation.

Perhaps at times our belief in ourselves is a little tenuous, and not as strong as we would like it to be. Yet, if we have faith in our vision and ourselves, we still can carry on and move forward, acting as if it will manifest.

We cannot be any other way and still create. If we do not have faith, then we would never start our next project or our next venture.

Do you see where you can have some more faith to move forward?

97.

....

WHEN WE ENVISION OUR FUTURE SELF, WE RISE TO THE VISION

How do we rise up higher? How do we grow to become more than we are today? We face challenges every day. How do we overcome and get past them in a more conscious way?

Perhaps it is by seeing our future selves. By imagining what we will be like in ten or fifteen years. Maybe if we can see ourselves, and others, as better than we are today we can grow into that image faster. By looking into the future of our lives maybe we can bring it into the present.

How would we handle this situation if it were fifteen years from now? Maybe just by asking the question we begin to think differently about what is in front of us.

By pointing our mind to our future self, we begin to create it today. Not by ignoring where we are. Not by thinking we are better than we are. But by leaning into the direction we are headed. By using our imagination to peer into the future we can bring it into the present.

Can it be that simple? That easy?

Perhaps.

We can only know for certain if we try. What are we struggling with today that our future self might be equipped to deal with? How would our future self approach this situation differently than we are today? It is an exercise in imagination. It is also an opportunity to play with life in a way that empowers us.

We all believe that we will be better in the future than we are now. Let's use that belief to help us in our day-to-day life. What choices would our future self make differently? What dreams would our future self have? What priorities would our future self work on? What perspective would our future self have that could aid us today? It's all there for the asking.

We may not get it exactly right, but who cares? At least we'll be moving in a direction we might not have thought about otherwise.

Let's use our future self to help use today.

Why not?

98.

....

THE FUTURE CALLS US FORTH
WITH OUR VISIONS

Sometimes we feel a pull in one direction or another. A certain project comes to mind and we feel drawn toward it. This vision is so compelling that we can't stop thinking about it.

This is a sign that the future is calling to us. It is calling to us to fulfill a destiny. It is calling to us to walk a certain path. It calls to our soul to be who we are becoming.

When the future reaches back into the past, it is sending a signal. It is providing a lighted path for us to follow. It already knows where we will end up and is guiding us there.

This is not about fate, but about possibilities. Deep in our core we know this is where we are to go. Our spirit is whispering to us to awaken. To bring our joy forward into the present.

That we have a vision does not mean everything will go smoothly or that there won't be great challenges along the way. Yet when we are on the path of our spirit's calling, there is a grace about it. There is a light that surrounds it. There is a peacefulness inside of us as we tread it.

Not everyone will answer the call from the future. Not everyone will fulfill their vision. Yet if more people at least walk the path of a vision, regardless of where theirs leads them, then everyone will realize it is okay to dream and follow a soul calling.

In creating from a vision, our example can serve as a light for others who feel drawn to their own vision. What a world we would be in if we all answered that call.

Is there a vision calling you forward? Do you have a vision that you are burning to fulfill?

99.

···

HOW WE FEEL ABOUT LIFE DEPENDS ON THE PROJECTIONS WE SEND OUT

We see things in life all the time that we are sure are real. How someone says something to us and the meaning behind it seem clear to us. Our memories are also filled with moments that we are certain happened a specific way. And it's true that all these life experiences actually happened, yet our memories of them are filled with our mental projections.

What our friend did was done "because they don't like us."

What our partner said was said "because they're mad at us."

Why our parents acted as they acted "because they are not proud of us."

We constantly think we know what is going on inside someone else's mind. Yet what we are doing is projecting our feelings and interpretations onto our experience.

Perhaps our friend was just in a rush and forgot to be polite.

Perhaps our partner got some bad news we don't know about and they are mad about it.

Perhaps our parents just learned that a friend of theirs died and they're upset over it.

How we interpret the world around us has less to do with the actual events and more about how we feel about ourselves. Do we feel deep inside that we're not good enough? Do the things we experience make us feel less than? Do we feel that there's something wrong with us? Do our relationships trigger those feelings? Do we feel that we don't deserve good things? Do we often feel the other person is taking advantage of us?

It's not so cut and dry.

Our perspective and self-image have a lot to do with it.

Perhaps when we get triggered, we can use this feeling as an opportunity to look inside ourselves. Perhaps when we feel someone is against us, we can check in and see if we are battling with ourselves. Perhaps instead of assuming it's always about the other person, we can take a step back and look for the thoughts and feelings we are projecting on them and claim them as our own.

As we being to recognize the projections we put on others, we realize that there is so much we are making up ourselves. As we learn to drop those projections, we see a clearer picture of what and who is before us.

Can you begin to recognize some of your own projections?

100.

....

THERE IS OFTEN A HUGE DIFFERENCE BETWEEN PERCEPTION AND TRUTH

Our perceptions are tricky things. We think we know what is going on, yet we only see it from our perspective. That conversation we had with our partner or the event that happened in another part of the world is open to our interpretation based on our perceptions.

In order to stay grounded, it is useful to ask ourselves a simple question. Is that really true? Is our perception or interpretation of a given situation actually true for other people and not just us? If a third party, someone not involved emotionally in it, saw or heard what went on, would they have the same conclusion as we do?

What we often think of as an objective fact is rarely so. The more we question our perceptions and our assumptions, the more we realize how much of our belief is opinion and not fact.

By asking "Is that really true?" it becomes obvious that even our own thoughts are interpretations. What is true for us today is not always true for everyone else. So, it is useful to double-check when we recognize there are assumptions and interpretations present.

Is that really true? If this question becomes part of our daily practice, we can catch our assumptions. We can catch other people's assumptions.

We can be humbler when presenting our opinions.

We can connect with people on a deeper level.

So, can you remember to turn this simple questions into a daily practice: *"Is that really true?"*

101.

····································

CLARITY OF INTENTION IS THE MOST POWERFUL FORCE OF NATURE

Intention is not just a whimsical thought. Not a daydream or a wish.

Intention is the energy we put into an action, a word, or a feeling. It is what makes the difference between creating an outcome of joy and one of misalignment.

Intention is how we create a world and a life by design, instead of by default. It is what makes our efforts powerful and effective.

Taking the time to sit and get clear about our intentions is one of the best investments of time, energy, and focus we can make. Meditating on a course of action is not wasted effort; it is essential. We need to do it to provide space for our thoughts so that we can think clearly.

Clarity of intention is one of the most powerful forces of nature.

Have you taken the time to set your intentions today?

102.

....

DISCERNMENT IS ABOUT
FEELING IT OUT

Most people think discernment is making the right choice. We use our logical minds to weigh the pros and cons and come up with the best choice. Yet discernment is much more than making rational decisions. It is making decisions based on how we feel about a given situation.

Often, there is not enough overt evidence to go in a particular direction. Let's say we've just met someone and we think they should be a good person because other people have said good things about them. Yet our impression, for no good reason, is that they are not trustworthy. Something just doesn't feel right. Maybe when we shook their hand, we got a chill.

Based on this discerning feeling, we think we should walk away. The trouble happens when we second guess ourselves and start thinking that we shouldn't be judgmental but should give the person a chance.

If we do, what happens? The person turns out to be the creep we felt they were yet had no backup evidence to prove.

Discernment means listening to feeling—our intuitive way of understanding that something is off—and taking it seriously. We don't have to know what is off, just that something feels off. Sometimes it can as subtle as an inflection in a person's voice or a look in their eye. Or maybe it's just an energetic hunch.

Trusting our feelings is the surest way to improve our discernment.

How can you use your feelings to improve your discernment?

103.

....

THE UNIVERSE SPEAKS TO US ALL THE TIME, WE JUST HAVE TO PAY ATTENTION

Messages come to us from the Universe every single day. They come to us in many forms. They show up in different aspects of our life. The important thing is to pay attention to them.

These messages may be ones of encouragement that come to us:

- By the right people showing up at the right time.
- By the unexpected phone call.
- By the new opportunity showing up.

We sometimes things these are just the results of the work we've done. And they are. And they also are more than that.

Why did things go so smoothly this time compared to the last? Why did business suddenly pick up even though we haven't done anything differently?

Pay attention. Do the circumstances of our life move us in a particular direction? Do they cause us to lean towards or away from a certain situation? Perhaps the Universe is trying to tell us something.

Perhaps life is speaking to us in the only way it can. Are we open to listening? Are our eyes opening to seeing? If we are not open, we usually don't see. If we are closed off to a possibility because of calling it "impossible," we usually don't get it.

Nothing is impossible for life. Yes, there are many paths before us. But when we pay attention to the signs around us, we know which one to take.

Are you paying attention to what the Universe is telling you?

104.

....

RELEASING CONTROL AND TRUSTING MORE ALLOWS LIFE TO SURPASS OUR IMAGINATION

We often get in trouble when we focus too much on control. The desire for control comes from more than fear. We look to control our circumstances, our environment, and our relationships because of something deeper. It comes from a profound lack of trust.

A lack of trust in ourselves. A lack of trust in the world. A lack of trust in life.

In our minds, we have good reasons for this lack of trust. Yet, if we look deeply into our heart, we want to trust more than anything else.

Making the effort to control everything in our lives is exhausting. It also leaves little room for life to bring us the unexpected. While that may sound comforting to us, it is also quite limiting. Life can surprise us with the most amazing adventures when we allow it to.

Giving up control is not about releasing our responsibilities in our lives. It is about trusting ourselves deeply that we can handle and thrive in any situation life brings us.

By trusting more and controlling less, we can allow amazing circumstances to develop. We can allow others to contribute more and truly create team efforts. We can lessen the stress in our lives and live more joyfully. We can start to have a happier journey throughout our lives.

Yes, control can be very comforting.

Is it worth it?

Can you release some control learn to trust more?

105.

....

THE CURE FOR JUDGMENT IS OWNING OUR OWN HUMANITY

It can be difficult not to judge others. It can take a lot of restraint not to make someone else wrong for what they did. Or for what they think.

Really, when we judge we are separating ourselves from others. Our judgments create barriers that protect us from getting too close. They even keep us from ever having to get close to the other person. We declare them bad, different, and not as good as we are.

For example, we might say, "They are a bigot, so we don't have to feel their pain," "They stole from us, so we don't have to see their need," "They hurt us, so we don't have to recognize their humanity."

Having compassion for those we feel judgment toward is not easy. It is a discipline that takes effort to develop. It also means having to recognize that people are merely people, and we all have faults. It means having to admit our own flaws, character defects, and transgressions.

We all have them. No one is above being human. We've all made mistakes and errors in our lives. Perhaps we have learned from them while others have not yet. Even so, we are more the same than we are different.

How can we continue to separate ourselves from our fellow human being, when we have done just as bad or worse? Are we really so pure? So great? So special?

We are all tainted in some way, and that is beautiful. Because that is what can bring us together. Without judgment or blame. Even for ourselves.

We are all human, one race, one people, one planet.

Where can you release judgment in your life? How can you see yourself as part of the greater whole?

106.

....

TO GET PAST THE NEED TO KNOW, WE MUST CULTIVATE TRUST

There are so many things we feel we need to know. For example, we may feel that we need to know our purpose life. We may feel that need to know who our soul mate is. We may feel that need to know what happens when we die. But all of these *needs* are not really *needs* at all.

Many of us live perfectly happy lives without knowing any of it. In fact, *knowing* these things will not necessarily help us to be any happier.

What if we don't like the answers?

What if we want to change them and can't?

Where would the mystery in life be if we knew all those answers?

Indeed, if we really knew everything that we thought we needed to know, would we not keep finding other things we felt we needed to know?

Knowing the answers does not give us a more fulfilled life. Knowing the answers does not automatically make us happier, healthier, or wiser.

The reason why is because the need to know comes from fear, not trust. Feeling a need to know is a symptom of the desire for security and certainty, and not based on love and acceptance. We want to know what we do not know because we feel knowing will make us safer. As if knowing the answer to all these questions will somehow make everything better for us. As if knowing will help us be less fearful.

Perhaps the biggest lesson in life is learning that we don't have to know everything. That not knowing is actually a great gift. That when we live with curiosity and trust, instead of fear and doubt. That we can "not know" and still be happy.

We can have our fears and not let them drive us. We can get past the need to know, and instead cultivate acceptance of what is. Cultivate trust in life. See all the events that led up to this moment and know that we are taken care of. Perhaps not the way we wanted—yet taken care of, nonetheless. Here we are. We survived, even when we didn't know how we would make it.

We don't know how we made it to this point in our lives. We also don't really know how tomorrow, next week, next month, or next year will go for us. Yet, as we trust, we are empowered to move forward and continue our journey in life.

So where can you trust more and know less in your own life?

107.

....

OUR ABILITY TO FOCUS IS OUR MOST MAGICAL SUPERPOWER

We all share a magical superpower. Although we may barely notice that we use it all the time, it is so strong that it creates worlds. This is the power of our focus.

The power to direct or mind or thoughts is extraordinary. We have all seen it in action. Whether it is something that benefits us or not, the more we focus on something, the larger it grows. We can focus on our pain and find more pain. We can focus on our joy and find more joy. It is up to us what we get to magnify. We get to choose what we focus on.

Do we focus on the solution or the challenge? Do we focus on our past, the future, or the present? And does what we focus on serve us in this moment?

One of the biggest mistakes we can make is to focus on something we don't want in our lives instead of focusing on what we really want (perhaps more health, more fun, or more prosperity). Because by focusing on it, we give it more power. More energy. More prominence in our lives.

It takes practice to be conscious with our focus. To recognize what it is we are actually giving power to. However, once we have that awareness, we can bring more choice to our lives. And choose to focus on something else. Or a different aspect of the situation.

There are always many ways to see the same situation. It all depends on what we are focusing on.

Are you aware of what you focus on in your life?

108.

························

THE BEST REASON TO DO THE HARD WORK IS WHAT WE LEARN IN THE PROCESS

When the time comes to step up, stand out, make some noise, and take a stand, we are all a little shy, a little awkward, and a little scared.

That's okay. It is scary to try something new, to push outside our comfort zone, and become the center of attention when we are not used to it.

Yet, if we are to make a difference, contribute, discover, and lead, we have to embrace that awkwardness and integrate it in as part of the process.

Nothing happens when we step back, don't take risks, and maintain the status quo. Yes, it's safer that way, and it leads us to just more of the same. But when we muster the courage to put ourselves out there, allow the spotlight to shine on us, and speak our truth, then we can have an impact.

All great work impacts us, sometimes in ways we don't understand. Sometimes the best reason for creating great work is merely to go through the process so we can learn to take the next step and become the example others need to feel comfortable in taking their next step.

Let's embrace the awkward stage, for soon it will be gone.

PART SEVEN

OUR WORLD

INSPIRATION, IMAGINATION, AND CONTRIBUTION

109.

································

THE BEGINNING OF WISDOM COMES WHEN WE REALIZE WE DON'T KNOW ANYTHING

Most of us think we're pretty smart. We've got a lot of things figured out. We've got a plan for our careers, our relationships, and our lives. Then life happens and, suddenly, all those plans go out the window.

Maybe it was a health challenge we didn't expect. Maybe it was something that happened to someone close to us. Maybe our industry suddenly collapsed, and we don't know what to do next. Slowly, but surely, over time we then begin to realize that we really don't know anything.

Our predictions of the future were all wrong. Our assumptions about relationships and family turned out to be more complicated than we expected. Our vision for our lives suddenly seems to be a fantasy.

Then we drop it all.

We drop our expectations. We drop our projections. We drop our certainty.

And that's when true wisdom begins.

When we come to the realization that we know absolutely nothing, we can begin to accept what is. When we stop our belief that we are the center and the master of the Universe, then the Universe can bring us magic. When we finally give up our egoic stance that we are so great and so smart, then we can start to find peace inside.

It doesn't happen overnight. It doesn't happen all at once. Yet, when it does happen, it feels like magic.

It feels like a relief.

We soften and then know that it is okay that we don't know anything.

So, where can you be humble in your life and know that you don't know?

110.

....

WHEN WE OPEN UP TO POSSIBILITIES, WE CAN SEE THE MAGIC OF LIFE

Sometimes, we crave to see evidence of magic in our lives. We want that something special to show up in a way we can see it, touch it, feel it. We want to see something we can't explain any other way.

At the same time, we are skeptical of magic and miracles. We have a hard time believing in unseen things. We feel that magic just doesn't happen for us.

Here's the thing. If we want magic to show up in our lives, we need to change. To change our perspective. To change our attitude. To be open to the possibility. If we would allow ourselves to be just a little more open, we would create space for magic to show up.

Sometimes the magic is all around us and we just don't see it. Small coincidences go unnoticed. There's the person who calls right when you are thinking about them. The 11:11 on the clock. The angel speaking to us in subtle ways. If we do not look for it, we do not see it.

Yet when we open our eyes, when we open our hearts to the magic of life itself, when we embrace the miracles that are all around us, we see and experience so much more magic.

What was once impossible is now possible. What was once unimaginable is now very real. And our lives become joyful knowing there is magic in them.

The shift is not an easy one, especially if we have spent a lifetime being skeptical and close-minded. To open up now is asking a lot of ourselves. Yet it is the only path we can take to have this desire fulfilled, for only those who believe in magic will see magic.

Real magic. Not sleight-of-hand tricks. The magic of life itself.

Have you been closed to magic?

Can you open up to seeing the magic in your own life?

....

111

FREEDOM LIES NOT IN THE EXTERNAL WORLD, BUT IN OUR INTERNAL LIMITLESSNESS

Being free with ourselves feels good. It may not be natural in our society, yet it is still an inherent desire, as to be free with ourselves is to be free from fear, free from concerns, and free from worry about what others will think.

Being free is not about living in a free country or an open society but about being free from our own internal bonds. It's about being free from our preconceptions and our biases and free from our assumptions and our nightmares.

There are levels and degrees of freedom. To have an absolutely free spirit is to allow our heart and soul to shine. Regardless of what anyone else thinks. Regardless of what anyone else does. Regardless of what anyone else says.

To be free to this degree, at the highest level, means to be so free on the inside that what's going on outside us is of little consequence. It means we have a free mind, heart, body, and soul.

It does not have to mean that we are free to do what we want, yet it does mean that we are free to think and feel what we want. We are free to choose the meaning we make in any given circumstance. We are free to feel what we choose to feel about ourselves and the world. No one can take that freedom away from us. No one can take the desire for freedom away from us. No one can take our free will away from us.

External choices may be limited, yet internal choices are always limitless.

In that limitlessness lies our freedom.

Where can you exercise more internal freedom regardless of your external circumstances?

112.

....

WE ARE SO MUCH MORE THAN THE SUM OF OUR PARTS

We have a heart, a head, a spirit, and a body, yet we are more than our heart, head, spirit, or body—and it makes a huge difference.

When challenges show up, we could respond using only one or two of these aspects of our being—or all four. We can try to think it through. We can meditate and pray on it until inspiration comes. We can look to our heart and seek connection and community with the people we know, like, and trust. We can rely on our body to take the physical actions necessary. We are not limited in how we respond. It never has to be one way over another or to the exclusion of the others. We are much more than the sum of our parts.

Indeed, when we call upon all of ourselves, our heart, our mind, our body, and our spirit, we can show up more fully to the challenge. By bringing the fullness of our being to meet the challenges and opportunities of our life, life gets better.

Our relationships get better.

Our business gets better.

Our health gets better.

We blossom and grow.

So why would we ever limit ourselves to being less than we are?

Yes, we are heart, mind, body, and spirit. And we are also so much more.

Are you bringing all of yourself to your challenges?

113.

....

EVOLUTION IS A CONSCIOUS CHOICE WE CAN MAKE EVERY DAY

How we evolve is not about our environment. It is not about our genetics. It is not about nature. It is about the stories we tell ourselves and the internal work we do.

We evolve when we are in pain and find a way to accept it. We evolve when we face our shadow and learn to befriend it. We evolve when we stop telling ourselves how we are not worth it and start acting like we are.

Change is a conscious choice. It happens when we make a decision and follow through.

Change is neither random nor linear. It happens organically, yet we can choose to resist it or flow with it.

The choice is always ours.

Here are some concrete examples. We can choose to learn about diverse people with an open heart, and thereby work to eliminate discrimination. We can choose to focus on peace, and thereby create a more peaceful world.

We can choose to ignore the problems we perceive and keep things the way they are.

Evolution is a conscious act. It happens when we make the effort to do something differently. To be a different person. To cultivate a sense of safety where there currently is a sense of fear.

There are challenges all around us—some big, some small. How we decide to respond to those challenges speaks to where we are in our evolution.

Are you happy with how you are evolving in your life?

Where are you choosing to evolve in your own life?

114.

....

WHEN WE USE OUR INTUITION, AMAZING THINGS HAPPEN

Our intuitive hunches may not work out all the time. Sometimes, we follow them, and in hindsight, make obvious mistakes. Yet our imperfect intuition guides us more accurately than our logic.

Why? Because following our intuition, once we've practiced following it, just feels better. Yes, it sometimes means ignoring the facts. Yes, it sometimes means not being able to explain ourselves. Yes, it sometimes even feels foolish in the face of other people's logical arguments. Yet, when we follow the feeling we receive from our intuition, it just feels right.

It feels right in our body because we are learning to trust our body's intelligence. We were taught to value the mind's intelligence above all else. This makes trusting the body more difficult. Yet, when we do, amazing things happen.

That person we felt wasn't quite trustworthy, turns out actually not to be trustworthy. That opportunity we took a chance on, because it felt right, eventually pays off big time. That relationship we were stuck in that didn't feel right finally ends so we can meet our life partner.

Our intuition is right far more than it is wrong. We just have to learn to trust it and use it more, like we would a muscle. It gets stronger with use.

Start paying attention to your own intuition. Recognize it. Test it. See where it leads you.

115.

WE ARE SPIRIT AND MATTER, AND BOTH ARE IMPORTANT

We often find two extremes in people. Some people are intensely concerned with the material world. Others are enthralled with spiritual issues. Matter and spiritual are two ends of a spectrum. To be on either end of the spectrum is to miss the point.

We are spiritual beings having a physical experience. Science had shown us that all matter is particles made of microscopic packets of energy. Yet, to our eyes, at the macro level, there is no "proof" that anything other than the physical world exists.

When we learn that our spirit—our energy and consciousness—is the creative source of the physical world, we can better appreciate both ends of the spectrum.

We live in physical bodies for a reason. We are real. And when we experience trauma or elation, that is also real. When our bodies die, that is real.

Yet, we are not only our bodies. We are not only our thoughts. We are not only our emotions. We are so much more— so much greater than any of that. And when we deny that our spiritual side is real, too, we disempower ourselves.

The same is true of denying our physical existence. When we deny our bodies, we deny our health. When we deny our health, we deny our ability to contribute to this world.

The density of the material world may be an illusion. Yet our experiences in the material world are real. Our choices are real. Our path is real.

It does not matter whether you believe it or not, the world still affects us.

So, let's stop ignoring whether spirit or matter is more important. Let's start to embody the magnificent creative that underlies who we are. Let's honor all life and not just the parts of life we treasure.

We are all part of a greater whole.

We are all brothers and sisters.

When will we start acting like it?

116.

·······································

BEING A RESPONSIBLE HUMAN MEANS BEING RESPONSIBLE TO LIFE ITSELF

Responsibility is a word that gets a lot of use.

We are responsible to our shareholders, our customers, our family, and our society. We are responsible to provide value, to contribute, and to be productive. We are also responsible for being honest, having integrity, and being true to ourselves. Ultimately though, our greatest responsibility is to life. We are responsible for supporting life and being supported by life.

We are responsible to the planet, and all the various forms of life on the planet. We are responsible for feeding ourselves—not just our body, but our spirit, our soul, our essence. We are also responsible for the energy we bring with us throughout the day.

Are we cheerful or depressed? Are we focused on solutions or problems? Are we supportive of those around us, or only concerned about ourselves?

That said, there's a lot of responsibility to go around, and it is not all ours. What is ours, however, is no one else's.

Let's be a little more responsible to life and a little less responsible for harming others.

Where can you be more responsible to yourself and not others?

117.

....

WITHOUT LIGHT THERE IS NO SHADOW

People often speak about doing "shadow work," healing their "shadow," and integrating their
"shadow." What we often don't think about is how real-world shadows indicate where there is a light source. Maybe psychologically, our shadow indicates something similar?

In the real-world, without light coming from a specific direction, there can be no shadow. As light shifts and changes its position, so too does the shadow it produces shift and change. We see this effect of movement in the shadows on a single sunny day. In the morning, our shadows are long. As the day progresses, the shadow shrinks, until the Sun is directly overhead, and then the shadow disappears altogether for a few minutes. As the Sun continues its route, the shadow reappears. At first it is small, and then is gets longer throughout the day, until the Sun sets. Then there is no more shadow until the next day.

So, perhaps we should pay more attention to how our inner light is shining, instead of how long the shadow of our repressed and denied thoughts and feelings is?

Better yet, perhaps as we shine light inside of ourselves, looking at all aspects and sides of ourselves in the full brightness of our light, we can come to love and accept all the scared parts of us hiding in the dark, who are afraid of how we will treat them.

Perhaps more kindness, acceptance, and awareness directed inwardly is all we need. When we are in full acceptance of ourselves, it could be as if the Sun is overhead— no shadow, only light.

Where can you embrace and love your own shadows?

118.

....

BY CHANGING OURSELVES, WE CHANGE OUR WORLD

Changing our surroundings is easy. We can pick up and move to a different building or a different town. We can change our job or our business. But unless we change ourselves, we will eventually end up in similar circumstances.

Like that friend of yours who always end up dating the same type of person. Or the relatives who always complains about their coworkers no matter where they are working.

Yes, sometimes a shift in our location is what we need to grow and expand. Then again, if we are expecting the change in environment to change our world completely, then we will be disappointed because our energy and internal state dictate what kind of people and situations unfold before us.

Our energy attracts a certain kind of partner. Our beliefs draw various opportunities and experiences to us. Our attitudes will determine how we respond to what is presented to us, which will lead to specific results. If we find that we constantly end up in the same type of situation, then it is about something within us, not the outside world.

When we change, *profoundly change* on a deep level, our world changes. Our friends change. Our family changes. Our boss changes. Our job/business/career changes.

It is a great opportunity and a source of empowerment that we can change ourselves, and by changing ourselves, change our world.

What do you want to change in yourself today?

119.

LET THE LIGHT OF OUR YEARS BE GREATER THAN OUR YEARS IN THE LIGHT

Growing older is not about growing old. As we accumulate years, we gain in so many ways. We gain experience, wisdom, and perspective. Yet the numbers on the calendar do not dictate our frame of mind, the energy in our heart, or the twinkle in our eye.

We have a choice—as we do with everything—to embrace, enjoy, and enliven our latter years with a youthful energy, an innocence, and an energy that says to the world we are always young at heart. Or we can choose to focus on all the loss, the bitterness, the deprivation we have experienced and make our world darker, decrepit, and depressing.

"Any day above ground is a good day," it has been said. As long we have breath, we can give more life, give more love, and give more light to the world around us.

Our days are numbered, and no one knows exactly how many we have. Let us live as if each day is the best day we have ever had, regardless of whether we have had few of them or many of them.

Let our smile, our heart, our words, and our energy contribute to the joy in the world, especially if it's our last day in the world.

What better way to be remembered?

120.

························

CONTRIBUTION IS ABOUT HOW WE FEEL WHEN WE GIVE BACK

Contribution is not really about other people. It is not about our community, our friends, or our world. Contribution is about finding meaning in something more than ourselves. It is about how we feel when we give back to the society that has given us so much.

Our contribution can be an effort as small as giving a charity or organization that is doing good work a few bucks. It also can be truly giving of ourselves, like donating our time and energy to a shelter or soup kitchen by showing up and pitching in with our two good hands.

There are many ways to contribute, not just time or money. We can contribute our influence or our resources. We can contribute our ideas, or our expertise.

The act of giving is more about how it makes us feel to give, than about being altruistic and gaining recognition. Of course, feeling good and altruism are not necessarily incompatible or exclusive.

The point is this: There is nothing wrong with doing the right thing because it makes us feel good. Indeed, isn't that the sign of an enlightened soul to take pleasure in helping others?

Where do you feel called to contribute?

Where can you find joy in helping others?

121.

······························

OUR STRUGGLE IS OUR OPPORTUNITY TO PRACTICE OUR WISDOM

It is common to get upset in the face of challenges. We may be annoyed or upset that we are still struggling. Yet these very struggles are great opportunities. They are our opportunities to grow. Our chance to put into practice all the things we have learned.

A struggle is a gift to become more conscious of how we are responding. They are moments of choice. Do we choose to respond out of anger or fear? Or do we choose to respond out of understanding and love?

Yes, we probably should love ourselves more, but this doesn't mean we have to stop loving others. Once we have taken care of ourselves, we can turn our attention to taking care of the needs of others.

Our choice is in how we become wiser in the moment. Our choice is in letting go of our reactions and instead learn to respond from a place of empowerment.

As we learn to respond with kindness and joy throughout our struggles, we will lift ourselves and others up. Coming at a challenge from a posture of gratitude and peace enables us to show up in the world in a manner that's supportive. Our trials and tribulations are an opportunity to take the spiritual understanding we have inside and bring it outside to practice what we believe.

To make manifest the world we say we want to live in.

It all starts and ends with us. The energy we bring to any situation determines more about the outcome of that situation than anything else. Especially in our interactions with people, it is not about winning or losing. It is not about getting what we want at the expense of another person. It is about how we feel when it is all over.

It is about how well we can sleep that night and how our heart feels when all is said and done. Anytime we come at life from the proper place, we feel better. If we know, deep inside, that we were aligned with a higher purpose and a higher way of being, we will be at peace inside.

We can smile to ourselves. We can laugh about it all—and if not right away, then in a few days, weeks, months, or years. We win when we come from our heart. We thrive when we feel the alignment to our true essence.

Our struggles and the trials are just opportunities to learn how aligned we truly are.

Do you have something you are struggling with to which you could bring more joy?

122.

....

SURRENDER IS ABOUT ALLOWING LIFE TO LEAD US

Surrender is not about giving up.

It is not about giving in.

It is not about quitting.

It is about allowing life to be our guide.

It is about listening to the whispers of the Universe.

It is about giving up control and expectation.

When we surrender, we release resistance. We stop forcing things to go a certain way. We allow a greater intelligence to show us the way.

We can surrender and still have our sovereignty. Still have choice. Still have agency in our lives.

Yet if we truly surrender to the ebb and flow of life, we begin to feel more at ease. Life become less hard. And without realizing it, we begin to receive more. More of what we want. More joy. More happiness. More abundance.

Ultimately, we are surrendering something deep within us. Something that is intimately connected to the fabric of the Universe that is below the level of our awareness. It is submerged within the depths of our soul and on the level of the fabric of life itself.

How do we surrender to this aspect of our self? By letting go of the need to be right. By letting go of the need to be first. By letting go of the need to be in control. By allowing what is to just be without judgment. By allowing what is to unfold as it wants to. By seeing the perfection in everything, even when it is not what we would choose.

Surrendering is a path to peace.

The sooner we surrender, the sooner we will be at ease.

Where in your life can you find more peace by surrendering?

....

123

WE ARE FLOW, NOT SOMETHING THAT EXPERIENCES FLOW

Being *in flow* is something we may strive for. That feeling of everything going right when it all seems so easy. Yet there seems to be confusion about how to get there or maintain that feeling. Perhaps part of the issue is that we don't really understand what it means to be in flow.

Of course, flow can mean different things to different people. For many of us, it is just a feeling that we recognize when we feel it, yet we have a hard time describing it. But the bigger confusion is if we think flow is something separate and apart from us. The image of a river flowing and how we have to jump into it so we can be carried away by the water comes to mind as an analogy for this conception.

Could there be a better way of understanding flow? I would contend that from an energetic perspective flow is not something distinct and separate from us.

Flow is what surrounds and engulfs us every moment of every day. We are flow, not something/someone that experiences flow.

When we are aware of being flow, we experience being present in a unique way. We flow in our lives, jobs, and relationships, in all the significant moments and the mundane moments in between. Even when we are in resistance to what is occurring, we are experiencing flow—just flow of a different nature.

What would happen if instead of wondering, *How do I get into flow?* you tried asking, *What flow am I experiencing now?*

124.

....

THE MOMENTS LIVED BEING TRULY PRESENT ARE THE MOST PRECIOUS OF ALL

What do we measure a life by? Do we measure it by the number of dollars earned? Do we measure it by the number of lives touches? Or can we stop measuring everything and just acknowledge that each life is precious?

We all contribute in our own way. We all add to the fullness that is life in this world. We all add to the richness that makes up the tapestry of creation. Regardless of how much money we have earned. Regardless of how many accomplishments we are credited with. Regardless of the races won.

The moments we live being truly present with another being are the most precious of all. In the end, a life lived with joy and compassion is the richest life of all.

Our value as an individual is not about who is the most productive. It is not about who makes the most deals. It is not about who has the largest, or smallest, family. Our energy, our presence, creates a unique impact on this planet. Everyone adds something to the mix.

If we were not here, things would be different. If we never existed, life would be unimaginably altered. From the poorest of the poor to the richest and most famous, we all have a place in this world. Our roles are different, our purposes diverse.

As we learn to revel in our differences and stop comparing ourselves to others, we start to live life more fully. When we focus on each moment as the precious gift it is, we become rich in experience.

How are you measuring your life?

125.

THE RICHNESS OF LIFE IS FOUND IN THE PRESENT MOMENT

Distraction is all around us. Our phones, our computers, and our lives all vie for our attention. The amazing technology that brings us together makes it harder to have time for ourselves to just sit and stare out the window. To just breathe and relax. To be at peace in the present moment. There is more connection, which means there are more people pulling on our attention. Our friends, relatives, coworkers, and bosses are trying to get to us. They all want something from us. Or perhaps it is our clients, or the vendors with whom we work. Instant access means people are expecting us to respond immediately.

The stress of daily life keeps increasing. We are constantly pulled somewhere where we are not, so we miss out on the richness that is the present.

All of life is lived here (where we are) and in the present moment, yet our minds habitually take us out of it or far away with our worry and our anxiety.

What will they think about me?

Will I get the contract?

Will he call me back?

Will this work out?

With all these thoughts running around in our heads, how do we stay present? How do we feel what is going on in our body? How do we find space to connect with our soul?

Taking time for ourselves is essential, not optional. Just as breathing is not optional.

We need time to feel our feelings. We need time to process all that is going on around. We need to take a moment to just sit back and let it all flow.

When we are present, we are not holding on to the past and we are not worrying about the future. When we are present, we are enjoying the full texture of life. The smell of the coffee. The sound of the wind. The taste of our food. The light of the Sun.

Breathe. Just take a moment and breathe. You don't have to answer the phone this minute. You don't have to respond immediately to every message. You don't have to distract yourself by going online. Take the time to be offline! Take the time to be with yourself.

What are you feeling? Where is this sensation in your body?

Connecting to ourselves brings us into the present moment.

It may take some practice. That's okay. Practice it. Be with it. The benefits of being present are beyond the relief of being distracted.

Sit. Breathe. Repeat.

How does that feel?

126.

....

IF YOU SEE SOMETHING TO CHANGE IN THE WORLD, IT IS A CALL TO MAKE THE CHANGE

It is not that unusual to hear someone mention that something is not working right or is missing. We see a problem or feel a lack and we believe that someone should do something about it. The mistake we make is in thinking that solving the problem or responding to the need is someone else's responsibility.

It is not.

If we see something missing in our life or something that is not as we would like it, there's a reason why we see it and someone else doesn't. Just because it is in our world, in our experience, does not mean that someone else will have the same experience.

Our experience is a call to action.

See something that can be done better? Great! Build a better mouse trap.

See something missing from the world that would contribute to it? Great! Make that contribution.

See an easier way for something to be accomplished? Great! Imagine how many other people could benefit from your insight.

The reason we see it and others don't is because this is the chance for us to step up and do something about it and make a difference.

Does this mean we have to do everything ourselves? No. And just because we see a need or how something can be done better, does not mean we have to do something about it alone. We can share our insight or vision with others, and for those whom it resonates with, ask them to join us.

We are the ones we have been waiting for. Let's not wait any longer. Time to do what life is calling us to do.

Do you hear life calling you?

Do you have a vision for how to make something better in the world?

When would now be a good time to start?

ACKNOWLEDGMENTS

I am deeply grateful for my publishing team led by Laura Rubinstein and Stephanie Gunning. They have guided me through the whole process from concept to a shining work of which I couldn't be prouder.

A huge shoutout to Teresa de Grosbois and the Evolutionary Business Council of thought leaders who have been there for me when I needed them the most and are truly a big part of my soul tribe.

I am in deep gratitude for Armand Bytton, my shamanic teacher, and Ian Pai, my mentor: Both have guided me through deep inner work. Their guidance and teachings are prevalent and woven throughout this book.

Finally, I would like to thank all of my past teachers, healers, and cohorts, who have traveled with me on this amazing journey. This path has led us all to places we never imagined!

RESOURCES

For more daily thoughts from Sam Liebowitz, The Conscious Consultant, visit: TheConsciousConsultant.com/blog.

Access Your Free Gift
Download a free digital audio meditation "Uncovering Your Unconscious Blocks to Abundance":
Links.TheConsciousConsultant.com/AbundanceAudio

Book a Session with Sam
Whether you are dealing with emotional, spiritual, or life challenges, Sam is available to support you.
TheConsciousConsultant.com/offerings/sessions

The Conscious Consultant Hour Show
Need more wisdom from Sam?
- Listen to his weekly show "The Conscious Consultant Hour" LIVE on Thursdays at 12 PM U.S. Eastern time: TalkRadio.nyc
- Listen 24/7 to the archive: TalkRadio.nyc/shows/the-conscious-consultant-hour
- Listen on your favorite podcasting app (Apple Podcasts, Google Podcasts, Spotify, Stitcher, and iHeartRadio): Linktr.ee/Samwyz

ABOUT THE AUTHOR

Sam Liebowitz, known as the Conscious Consultant, is a twenty-seven-year veteran entrepreneur in the human potential and empowerment space. For more than ten years he has owned and operated Double Diamond Wellness, Inc., in the heart of Manhattan. There, Sam provides coaching, business mentoring, and healing services. He is also the owner of TalkRadio.NYC and has been hosting and producing broadcast-quality internet radio shows since 2010. Sam has dedicated his life and work to creating openings where people harness their superpowers and create an abundant, fulfilling, sustainable business, career, and life.